Captivating

OTHER BOOKS BY JOHN ELDREDGE

Love and War
(with Stasi Eldredge)

Wild at Heart

Fathered by God

Walking with God

Waking the Dead

Epic

Desire

The Sacred Romance
(Coauthored with Brent Curtis)

Captivating

Unveiling the Mystery *of a* *Woman's Soul*

JOHN AND STASI ELDREDGE

THOMAS NELSON
Since 1798

NASHVILLE DALLAS MEXICO CITY RIO DE JANEIRO

Published in Nashville, TN, by Thomas Nelson. Thomas Nelson is a registered trademark of Thomas Nelson, Inc.

Published in association with Yates & Yates, LLP, Attorneys and Counselors, Orange, California.

Thomas Nelson, Inc., titles may be purchased in bulk for educational, business, fund-raising, or sales promotional use. For information, please e-mail SpecialMarkets@ThomasNelson.com.

Unless otherwise noted, Scripture quotations are from the HOLY BIBLE: NEW INTERNATIONAL VERSION®. © 1973, 1978, 1984 by International Bible Society. Used by permission of Zondervan Publishing House. All rights reserved.

Scripture quotations noted *Alter* are from *Genesis: Translation and Commentary.* © 1996 by Robert Alter.

Scripture quotations noted NLT are from the *Holy Bible,* New Living Translation, © 1996. Used by permission of Tyndale House Publishers, Inc., Wheaton, Illinois 60189. All rights reserved.

Scripture quotations noted NASB are from the NEW AMERICAN STANDARD BIBLE®, © The Lockman Foundation 1960, 1962, 1963, 1968, 1971, 1972, 1973, 1975, 1977, 1995. Used by permission. (www.Lockman.org)

Scripture quotations noted NKJV are from THE NEW KING JAMES VERSION. © 1979, 1980, 1982 by Thomas Nelson, Inc. Used by permission. All rights reserved.

ISBN 978-1-4002-0282-9 (revised)
ISBN 978-1-4002-8101-5 (IE)

Library of Congress Cataloging-in-Publication Data

Eldredge, John.
    Captivating / John and Stasi Eldredge.
    p. cm.
    ISBN: 978-0-7852-6469-9 (HC)
    ISBN: 978-0-7852-8909-8 (TP)
    ISBN: 0-7852-2325-8 (SE)
    1. Christian women—Religious life. I. Eldredge, Stasi. II. Title.
    BV4527.E435 2005
    248.8'43—dc22

2004028651

Printed in the United States of America
10 11 12 13 QG 5 4

To the captivating women we
are blessed to call our friends.

Contents

❧

Introduction

*N*ow we are on holy ground.

Writing a book for men (*Wild at Heart*) was a fairly straight-forward proposition. Not that men are simpletons. But they *are* the less complicated of the two genders trying to navigate love and life together. Both men and women know this to be true. The mystery of the feminine heart was meant to be a good thing, by the way. A source of joy. Yet it has become a source of shame—women almost universally feel that they are "too much" and "not enough." At the same time. (Which is crazy-making.) And men tend to pull away from the deeper waters of a woman's soul, unsure of what they will find there or how to handle it. And so we have missed the treasure that is the heart of a woman, missed the richness femininity was meant to bring to our lives, missed the way it speaks to us of the heart of God.

Rest assured—this is not a book about all the things you are fail-ing to do as a woman. We're tired of those books. As a new Christian, the first book I (Stasi) picked up to read on godly femininity I threw across the room. I never picked it up again. In the thirty years since, I have only read a few I could wholeheartedly recommend. The rest drive me crazy. Their messages to women make me feel as though, "You are not the woman you ought to be—but if you do the follow-ing ten things, you can make the grade. Maybe." They are, by and large, soul-killing. But femininity cannot be prescribed in a formula. There is no "one size fits all" pattern for God's women.

We have women friends who love tea parties and china, and friends who break out in hives at the thought of them. We have women friends who love to hunt, bow hunt even. Women who love to entertain and women who don't. Women who are professors, moms, doctors, nurses, missionaries, dentists, homemakers, therapists, chefs, artists, poets, rock climbers, triathletes, secretaries, salespeople, and social workers. Beautiful women, all.

So—is a true woman Cinderella or Joan of Arc? Mary Magdalene or Oprah? How do we recover essential femininity without falling into stereotypes, or worse, ushering in more pressure and shame upon our readers? That is the last thing a woman needs. And yet, there *is* an essence that God has given to every woman. We share something deep and true, down in our hearts. So we venture into this exploration of femininity by way of the *heart*. What is at the core of a woman's heart? What are her desires? What did we long for as little girls? What do we still long for as women? And how does a woman begin to be healed from the wounds and tragedies of her life?

Sometime between the dreams of your youth and yesterday, something precious has been lost. And that treasure is your heart, your priceless feminine heart. God has set within you a femininity that is powerful and tender, fierce and alluring. No doubt it has been misunderstood. Surely it has been assaulted. But it is there, your true heart, and it is worth recovering. You *are* captivating.

So we invite you to take a journey with us, a journey of discovery and healing. For your heart is the prize of God's Kingdom, and Jesus has come to win you back for himself—all of you. To help your journey, we've written *Captivating: A Guided Journal.* You might want to use it as you read this book. And gather a group of women and go through it together! We pray that God will use this book in your life, in your heart, to bring healing, restoration, joy, and life! And if God does that, it will be cause for a wonderful celebration. With teacups and china. Or paper plates. Whatever. One day we will all celebrate together. In anticipation and hope, may this little book draw you closer to God's heart—and your own.

FIVE YEARS LATER

It has been five years since John and I wrote *Captivating: Unveiling the Mystery of a Woman's Soul.* The stories that have poured in over that time are breathtaking. What God has done for many, many women has been . . . glorious. He is setting his daughters free to be the women they are created to be. He is transforming hearts and minds and lives and families and communities and nations.

There is more to be done. More to be known. More to be healed. More to be released. More love to receive and more love to pour out. People today are desperate for meaning. They long to know that it is possible to live a life that matters. They are hungry for truth and dying of thirst for the Living Water. There is no greater mission on earth than to be part of God's great invasion and bring it to them; bring Jesus to them! But first, always first, we must bring *ourselves* to Jesus.

I love the story in Mark 5 of the woman with the issue of blood who out of *her* desperate need pushes through the throngs of people surrounding Jesus in order to touch the hem of his garment and be healed. You remember how it went. She had been bleeding for twelve years. She had spent all she had on the many doctors and treatments available to her. None of it had helped. In fact, she had only gotten worse. Now, broke and heartbroken, she has an unlooked for opportunity.

Jesus has come to her town. He is at this moment passing by. It is not lawful for her, a bleeding woman, to be gathered with other people. But she is dying. And she doesn't want to be. So against all odds and against the law, she presses *through* the crowd and presses *in* to Jesus. She reaches out with all the strength she yet possesses and touches him and is instantly *healed*.

Wow. Let that sink in for just a moment. She is instantly healed. This story is one of the lost treasures of the gospel.

The Bible tells us that Jesus never changes (Heb. 13:8). "Jesus Christ is the same yesterday, today and forever." Jesus still has the power to heal us as women, to touch *us*, to restore us in our places of deepest need. And we all have need. All of us. In fact, some of us have been bleeding much longer than twelve years.

What do you long for Jesus to do for you? What places in your heart are crying out for healing? Where have you lost hope? What do you need to press into Jesus for?

We want to encourage you to do just that. As you read this book, ask him! Press into him! Ask Jesus to come for *your* heart. He loves to do that. In fact, it is why he came.

CHAPTER ONE

The Heart of a Woman

Sometimes it's hard to be a woman.
—TAMMY WYNETTE

He saw that Fatima's eyes were filled with tears.
"You're crying?"
"I'm a woman of the desert," she said, averting her face.
"But above all, I'm a woman."
—PAULO COELHO

You belong among the wildflowers
You belong in a boat out at sea
You belong with your love on your arm
You belong somewhere you feel free.
—TOM PETTY

Let's do it." Dusk was settling in. The air was cool, fragrant with pine and sage, and the swiftly moving river beckoned. We were camping in the Tetons, and it so happened that our canoe was on top of the car. "Let's put in." John looked at me as if I had lost my mind. In less than twenty minutes night would be upon us and the river and the woods. All would be pitch black. We'd be on the river, alone, with only a general idea of which way to go (down), where to take out (head for the road), and a long walk back to the car. Who knew what dangers lay out there? He looked again at me, looked at our young sons, and then said, "Okay!" We sprang into action.

The evening was stunning. The river's graceful movements caused the water's colors to shift from cobalt to silver to black. No other person was in sight. We had Oxbow Bend to ourselves. In record time we had the canoe in the river; life vests securely fastened, paddles at the ready, boys installed, and off we went, a race to drink as deeply of as much beauty as possible, together.

An old wooden bridge hung low across the river; its broken remains looked as though they would collapse at the next strong breeze. We had to duck to pass underneath. Carefully, we navigated the winding channels of the Snake—John in back, me in front, our three boys in between, full of wonder and delight. As the stars began to come out, we were like the children present at the creation of Narnia—the sky so clear, the stars so close. We held our breath as one fell slowly, slowly across the sky and disappeared.

A beaver slapped the river, the sound like a rifle shot, frightening two ducks into flight, but all we could see between the darkened water and sky were the white ripples of their wake, like synchronized water-skiers. Owls began their nightly calls in the woods above, joined by sandhill cranes along the shore. The sounds were familiar, yet otherworldly. We whispered to one another about each new wonder, as the paddles dipped almost but not quite silently in and out of the water.

Night fell. Time to take out. We planned to go ashore along a cove closest to the road so we wouldn't have to walk too far to find our car. We didn't dare try to take out where we had put in . . . that would require paddling against the current with little ability to see where we were going.

As we drifted toward the bank, a bull moose rose from the tall grasses, exactly where we had planned to come ashore. He was as dark as the night; we could see him only because he was silhouetted against the sky, jagged mountains behind. He was huge. He was gorgeous. He was in the way. Blocking the only exit we had. More people are killed in national parks by moose than by any other animal. Remarkable speed, seventeen hundred pounds of muscle and antlers, and total unpredictability make them dangerous indeed. It would take about two seconds for him to hit the water running and capsize our canoe. We could not pass.

The mood changed. John and I were worried now. There was only one alternative to this way out, now closed to us, and that was paddling back upriver in what had become total darkness. Silently, soberly, we turned the canoe and headed up, searching for the right channel that would keep us out of the main current. We hadn't planned on the adventure taking that turn, but suddenly, everything was required. John must steer with skill; I must paddle with strength. One mistake on our part and the strong current would force the canoe broadside, fill it, and sweep our boys off downriver into the night.

It was glorious.

We did it. He did. I did. We rose to the challenge working together, and the fact that it required all of me, that I was in it with my family and for my family, that I was surrounded by wild, shimmering beauty and it was, well, kind of *dangerous*, made the time . . . transcendent. I was no longer Stasi. I was Sacagawea, Indian Princess of the West, a valiant and strong woman.

A Woman's Journey

I'm trying to remember when I first knew in my heart that I was no longer a girl, but had become a woman. Was it when I graduated from high school or college? Did I know it when I married? When I became a mother? I am forty-five years old as I write this, but there remain places in my heart that still feel so very young. As I think back on what would be considered rites of passage in my life, I understand why my journey has felt so unguided, uncertain. The day I started my period, my family embarrassed me at the dinner table by breaking out in song, "This girl is a woman, now . . ." Hmmmm. I didn't *feel* any different. All I felt was mortified that they *knew*. I stared at my plate, suddenly fascinated by corn.

The day I got my first bra, a training bra, the kind with stretchy material over the front, one of my sisters pulled me into the hallway where, to my horror, my father stood at the ready to take my picture. They said I would laugh about it later. (I haven't.) Like so many other women I was left alone to navigate my way through adolescence, through my changing and awakening body, a picture of my changing and awakening heart. No counsel was given for the journey into womanhood. I *was* encouraged, however, to eat less. My father pulled me aside and told me, "No boy will love you if you're fat."

I joined the feminist movement in college, searching, as so many women did in the '70s, for a sense of self. I actually became director of the Women's Resource Center at a liberal state university in California. But no matter how much I asserted my strength and independence as a woman ("hear me roar"), my *heart* as a woman remained empty. To be told when you are young and searching that "you can be anything" is not helpful. It's too vast. It gives no direction. To be told when you are older that "you can do anything a man can do" isn't helpful either. I didn't want to be a man. What does it mean to be a *woman?*

And as for romance, I stumbled through that mysterious terrain with only movies and music as a guide. Like so many women I know, I struggled alone through the mess of several broken hearts. My last year in college, I fell in love for real, and this young man truly loved me back. John and I dated for two and a half years and then became engaged. As we made wedding plans, my mother gave me a rare bit of counsel, in this case, her marriage advice. It was twofold. First, love flies out the window when there's no pork chop on the table. And second, always keep your kitchen floor clean; it makes the whole house look better. I caught her drift. Namely, that my new position as "wife" centered in the kitchen, making the pork chops and cleaning up after them.

I somehow believed that upon saying, "I do," I would be magically transformed into Betty Crocker. I imagined myself baking fresh bread, looking flushed and beautiful as I removed the steaming loaves from the oven. No matter that I hadn't cooked but five meals in my entire life, I set about preparing dinners, breakfasts even, with determination and zeal. After two weeks of this, I lay on the couch despondent, announcing that I didn't know what was for dinner and that John was on his own. Besides, the kitchen floor was dirty. I had failed.

My story is like most women's stories—we've received all sorts of messages but very little help in what it means to become a woman and very little guidance as to what a real woman even is. As one young woman recently wrote us,

> I remember when I was ten asking myself as well as older females in my life how a woman of God could actually be confident, scandalous, and beautiful, yet not portray herself as a feminist Nazi or an insecure I-need-attention emotional whore. How can I become a strong woman without becoming harsh? How can I be vulnerable without drowning myself in my sorrow?

There seems to be a growing number of books on the *masculine* journey—rites of passage, initiations, and the like—many of them

5

helpful. But there has been precious little wisdom offered on the path to becoming a woman. Oh, we know the *expectations* that have been laid upon us by our families, our churches, and our cultures. There are reams of materials on what you *ought* to do to be a good woman. But that is not the same thing as knowing what the journey toward becoming a woman involves, or even what the goal really should be.

The church has not been a big help here. No, that's not quite honest enough. The church has been part of the problem. Its message to women has been primarily, "You are here to serve. That's why God created you: to serve. In the nursery, in the kitchen, on the various committees, in your home, in your community." Seriously now—picture the women we hold up as models of femininity in the church. They are sweet, they are helpful, and their hair is coiffed; they are busy, they are disciplined, they are composed, and they are *tired.*

Think about the women you meet at church. They're trying to live up to some model of femininity. What do they "teach" you about being a woman? What are they saying to us through their lives? Like we said, you'd have to conclude that a godly woman is . . . tired. And guilty. We're all living in the shadow of that infamous icon, "The Proverbs 31 Woman," whose life is so busy I wonder, when does she have time for friendships, for taking walks, or reading good books? Her light never goes out at night? When *does* she have sex? Somehow she has sanctified the shame most women live under, biblical proof that yet again we don't measure up. Is that supposed to be godly—that sense that you are a failure as a woman?

UNSEEN, UNSOUGHT, AND UNCERTAIN

I know I am not alone in this nagging sense of failing to measure up, a feeling of not being good enough *as a woman.* Every woman I've ever met feels it—something deeper than just the sense of failing at what she does. An underlying, gut feeling of failing at who she *is*. *I am not enough*, and *I am too much* at the same time. Not pretty enough, not thin enough, not kind enough, not gracious enough, not disciplined enough. But too emotional, too needy, too sensitive, too strong, too opinionated, too messy. The result is Shame, the universal companion of women. It haunts us, nipping at our heels, feeding on our deepest fear that we will end up abandoned and alone.

After all, if we were better women—whatever *that* means—life wouldn't be so hard. Right? We wouldn't have so many struggles; there would be less sorrow in our hearts. Why is it so hard to create meaningful friendships and sustain them? Why do our days seem so unimportant, filled not with romance and adventure but with duties and demands? We feel *unseen*, even by those who are closest to us. We feel *unsought*—that no one has the passion or the courage to pursue us, to get past our messiness to find the woman deep inside. And we feel *uncertain*—uncertain what it even means to be a woman; uncertain what it truly means to be feminine; uncertain if we are or ever will be.

Aware of our deep failings, we pour contempt on our own hearts for wanting more. Oh, we long for intimacy and for adventure; we long to be the Beauty of some great story. But the desires set deep in our hearts seem like a luxury, granted only to those women who get their acts together. The message to the rest of us— whether from a driven culture or a driven church—is "try harder."

The Heart of a Woman

And in all the exhortations we have missed the most important thing of all. We have missed the *heart* of a woman.

And that is not a wise thing to do, for as the Scriptures tell us, the heart is central. "Above all else, guard your heart, for it is the wellspring of life" (Prov. 4:23). Above all else. Why? Because God knows that our heart is core to who we are. It is the source of all our creativity, our courage, and our convictions. It is the fountainhead of our faith, our hope, and of course, our love. This "wellspring of life" within us is the very essence of our existence, the center of our being. Your heart as a woman is the most important thing about you.

Think about it: God created you *as a woman.* "God created man in his own image . . . male and female he created them" (Gen. 1:27). Whatever it means to bear God's image, you do so *as a woman.* Female. That's how and where you bear his image. Your feminine heart has been created with the greatest of all possible dignities—as a reflection of God's own heart. You are a woman to your soul, to the very core of your being. And so the journey to discover what God meant when he created woman in his image— when he created *you* as his woman—that journey begins with your heart. Another way of saying this is that the journey begins with *desire.* The desires that God has placed into our hearts are clues as to who we really are and the role that we are meant to play. Many of us have come to despise our desires or at least try to bury them. They have become a source of pain or shame. We are embarrassed of them. But we don't need to be. The desires of our heart bear a great glory because, as we will detail further in the next chapter, they are precisely where we bear the image of God. We long for certain things because *he* does!

Look at the games that little girls play, and if you can, remember what you dreamed of as a little girl. Look at the movies women love. Listen to your own heart and the hearts of the women you know. What is it that a woman wants? What does she dream of? Think again of women like Tamar, Ruth, Rahab—not very "churchy" women, but women held up for esteem in the Bible. We think you'll find that every woman in her heart of hearts longs for three things: to be romanced, to play an irreplaceable role in a great adventure, and to unveil beauty. That's what makes a woman come alive.

TO BE ROMANCED

I will find you.
No matter how long it takes, no matter how far—I will find you.
—NATHANIEL TO CORA IN *THE LAST OF THE MOHICANS*

One of my favorite games growing up was "kidnapped and rescued." I know many little girls who played this—or wished they had. To be the beauty, abducted by the bad guys, fought for and rescued by a hero—some version of this had a place in all our dreams. Like Sleeping Beauty, like Cinderella, like Maid Marian, or like Cora in *The Last of the Mohicans*, I wanted to be the heroine and have my hero come for me. Why am I embarrassed to tell you this? I simply loved feeling wanted and fought for. This desire is set deep in the heart of every little girl—and every woman. Yet most of us are ashamed of it. We downplay it. We pretend that it is less than it is. We are women of the twenty-first century after all—strong, independent, and capable, thank you very much. Uh-huh . . . and who is buying all those romance novels?

Think about the movies you once loved and the movies you love now. Is there a movie for little girls that doesn't have a handsome prince coming to rescue his beloved? *Sleeping Beauty, Snow White, The Little Mermaid.* A little girl longs for romance, to be seen and desired, to be sought after and fought for. So the Beast must win Beauty's heart in *Beauty and the Beast.* So in the gazebo scene in *The Sound of Music*, the Captain finally declares his love to Maria by moonlight and song and then, a kiss. And we sigh. Isn't something stirred in you when Edward, *finally*, returns at the end of *Sense and Sensibility* to proclaim his love for Elinor? "Then . . . you're not . . . not married?" she asks, nearly holding her breath. "No," he says. "My heart is . . . and always will be . . . yours." Or how about when Friedrich returns for Jo at the end of *Little Women*? Or the sunset scene at the bow of the *Titanic*? And we can't forget *Braveheart*, how William Wallace pursued Murron with flowers and notes and invitations to ride. She is captured by his love, riding off bareback with him in the rain. (Come now. Wouldn't *you* want to ride through the Scottish Highlands with a man like Mel Gibson?)

When John and I began to "date," I had just come out of a three-year relationship that left me wounded, defensive, and gun-shy. John and I had been friends for many years, but we never seemed to connect in the romance department. I would like him, and he would want to remain "just friends." He would feel more for me and I would not for him. You get the picture. Until one autumn after he had become a Christian, and I was desperately seeking, our spiritual journeys, and the desires of our hearts, finally met.

John wrote me letters, lots of letters. Each one filled with his love for God and his passion for me, his desire for me. He spent hours carving a beautiful heart out of manzanita wood, then attached it to a delicate chain and surprised me with it. (I still cherish the necklace.) I came out to my car after my waitressing shift ended to find his poetry underneath my windshield. Verses written for me, to me! He loved me. He saw me and knew me and pursued me. I loved being romanced.

When we are young, we want to be precious to someone—especially Daddy. As we grow older, the desire matures into a longing to be pursued, desired, wanted as a woman. "Why am I so embarrassed by the depth of my desire for this?" asked a young friend just the other day. We were talking about her life as a single woman, and how she loves her work but would much rather be married. "I don't want to hang my life on it, but still, I yearn." Of course. You're a woman.

Now, being romanced isn't all that a woman wants, and John and I are certainly not saying that a woman ought to derive the meaning of her existence from whether or not she is being or has been romanced by a man . . . but don't you see that you *want* this? To be desired, to be pursued by one who loves you, to be someone's priority? Most of our addictions as women flare up when we feel that we are not loved or sought after. At some core place, maybe deep within, perhaps hidden or buried in her heart, every woman wants to be seen, wanted, and pursued. We want to be romanced.

AN IRREPLACEABLE ROLE IN A GREAT ADVENTURE

When I was a little girl, I used to love World War II movies. I imagined myself being in them. I dreamed of growing up, braiding my hair, and then tucking it up under my helmet. I planned to disguise my gender so that I could join in. I sensed that the men in these movies were part of something heroic, valiant, and worthy. I longed to be a part of it too. In the depths of my soul, I longed to be a part of something large and good; something that required all of me; something dangerous and worth dying for.

There is something fierce in the heart of a woman. Simply insult her children, her man, or her best friend and you'll get a taste of it. A woman is a warrior too. But she is meant to be a warrior in a uniquely feminine way. Sometime before the sorrows of life did their best to kill it in us, most young women wanted to be a part of something grand, something important. Before doubt and accusation take hold, most little girls sense that they have a vital role to play; they want to believe there is something in them that is needed and needed desperately.

Think of Sarah from *Sarah, Plain and Tall.* A man and his

young children need her; their world is not right until she becomes a part of it. She brings her courage and her creativity to the West and helps to tame it. We are awed by the nurses in *Pearl Harbor*, how in the midst of a horrifying assault they bring their courage and strength to rescue the lives of hundreds of men. The women in *The Lord of the Rings* trilogy are valiant and beautiful—women like Arwen, Galadriel, and Éowyn change the fate of Middle Earth. And what about women like Esther and Mary and Ruth? They were biblical characters who had irreplaceable roles in a Great Story. Not "safe" and "nice" women, not merely "sweet," but passionate and powerful women who were beautiful *as* warriors.

Why do I love remembering the story of canoeing in the dark beauty of the Tetons so much? Because I was needed. *I* was needed. Not only was I needed, but like Arwen, I was irreplaceable. No one else in that canoe could have done what I did.

Women love adventures of all sorts. Whether it be the adventure of horses (most girls go through a horse stage) or white-water rafting, going to a foreign country, performing onstage, having children, starting a business, or diving ever more deeply into the heart of God, we were made to be a part of a great adventure. An adventure that is *shared*. We do not want the adventure merely for adventure's sake but for what it requires of us *for* others. We don't want to be alone in it; we want to be in it *with* others.

Sometimes the idea of living as a hermit appeals to all of us. No demands, no needs, no pain, no disappointments. But that is because we have been hurt, are worn out. In our heart of hearts, that place where we are most *ourselves*, we don't want to run away for very long. Our lives were meant to be lived with others. As echoes of the Trinity, we remember something. Made in the image of a perfect relationship, we are relational to the core of our beings and filled with a desire for transcendent purpose. We long to be an irreplaceable part of a shared adventure.

BEAUTY TO UNVEIL

The king is enthralled by your beauty.
—PSALM 45:11

Lovely little six-year-old Lacey was visiting our ministry outpost the other day, going from office to office, swinging on the doorframe, and asking with a smile, "Would you like to hear my song?" Her faced kissed by the sun with charming freckles, two front teeth missing, and eyes dancing with merriment, who could refuse her? She didn't really care if she was an interruption. I doubt the thought crossed her mind. She sang her newly made-up song about puppies and kitties, fully expecting to be delighted in, then skipped down the hall to grace the occupant of the next office. She was like a ray of summer sun or, better, a garden fairy, flitting from office to office. She was a little girl in her glory, unashamed in her desire to delight and be delighted in.

It's why little girls play dress up. Little boys play dress up too, but in a different way. Our sons were cowboys for years. Or army men. Or Jedi knights. But they never once dressed up as bridegrooms, fairies, or butterflies. Little boys do not paint their toenails. They do not beg to get their ears pierced. (Some teenaged boys do, but that is another story.) Little boys don't play dress up with Mommy's jewelry and high heels. They don't sit for hours and brush each other's hair.

Remember twirling skirts? Most little girls go through a season when they will not wear anything if it does not twirl (and if it sparkles, so much the better). Hours and hours of endless play result from giving little girls a box filled with hats, scarves, necklaces, and clothes. Dime store beads are priceless jewels; hand-me-down pumps are glass slippers. Grandma's nightie, a ballroom gown. Once dressed, they dance around the house or preen in front of a mirror. Their young hearts intuitively want to know they are lovely.

13

Captivating

Some will ask with words, "Am I lovely?" Others will simply ask with their eyes. Verbal or not, whether wearing a shimmery dress or covered in mud, all little girls want to know. As a young songwriter recently wrote,

> *I want to be beautiful*
> *And make you stand in awe*
> *Look inside my heart*
> *And be amazed*
> *I want to hear you say*
> *Who I am is quite enough*
> *I just want to be worthy of love*
> *And beautiful.*
>
> —BETHANY DILLON, "BEAUTIFUL"

Last summer John and I attended a ball at the beautiful, historic Broadmoor Hotel. It was a stunning affair. Black tie. Candlelight. Dinner. Dancing. You name it. The courtyard where the hors d'oeuvres were served was filled with fresh flowers, flowing fountains, and the music of a gifted pianist. It was an evening long planned for. For weeks—no, *months* ahead of the affair—I, like every other woman who attended, asked the all-important question: "What will I wear?" (As the special night drew closer, I also wondered if it was possible to lose twenty pounds in seven days.)

The evening turned out to be glorious. The weather was perfect. Every detail attended to and lovely. But the highlight by far was the women. Above the sound of the splashing water from the fountains, even above the music that floated through the air, was the sound of delighted exclamations. "You look beautiful!" "You are gorgeous!" "What an amazing dress!" "How lovely you are!" We were delighting in each other's beauty and enjoying our own. We were playing dress up for real and *loving* it.

14

These women were normal women, women just like you and me. Women you would run into at the bank or the grocery store or the office. Women whose battles against acne have left their faces marked and their souls scarred. Women whose struggle with their weight has been the bane of their lives. Women who always felt their hair was too thin, too thick, too straight, or too curly. Ordinary women, if there is such a thing. But women who, at least for a few hours this night, took the risk of revealing their beauty. Perhaps better, whose beauty was *unveiled.*

Think of your wedding day—or the wedding day you dream of. How important is your dress as a bride? Would you just grab the first thing in your closet, throw on "any old thing"? A friend of ours is getting married in six months. Now, this young woman has seen her share of boys and heartbreaks. Her tale of beauty has many hurts to it. But as she told us about trying on wedding dresses and finding just the right dress, the weariness faded away, and she was radiant. "I felt like a princess!" she said, almost shyly. Isn't that what you dreamed of?

One little girl, who is being raised in a home where her feminine heart is welcomed, told her mother about a wonderful dream she had.

My daughter Emma—nearly six years old—came to me all aglow this morning. She lay at my feet on my bed all stretched out as if she hadn't a care in the world. "Mommy," she said, "I had a wonderful dream last night." "What was it about?" I asked. "I was a Queen," she answered. And as she did her cheeks blushed pink. "Really!" I replied. "What happened in your dream?" "I was wearing a long, beautiful dress," she said with hands gesturing downward, flowing. "Was there anything on your head?" I wondered aloud. "Yes, a crown." "Hmmmm, why was that such a wonderful dream?" "I just love feeling that way!" "What way?"

And with a sigh she spoke one word . . . "Beauty." (Emma's
Dream, as told to her mother)

The desire to be beautiful is an ageless longing. My friend Lilly
is in her mideighties. As she descended the stairs of her home one
Christmas season, I was captured by her beauty. She was wearing a
green corduroy jumper with a white turtleneck that had little candy
canes all over it. I said, "Lilly, you look lovely!" Her face lit up, wrin-
kles and age spots disappearing as she put her hands out at her sides
like a ballerina and did a delightful little twirl. She was no longer
eighty—she was ageless. God has set eternity in our hearts. The
longing to be beautiful is set there as well.

Now, we know that the desire to be beautiful has caused many
women untold grief (how many diets have you been on?). Countless
tears have been shed and hearts broken in its pursuit. As Janis Ian
sang, "I learned the truth at seventeen, that love was meant for
beauty queens, and high school girls with clear-skinned smiles."
Beauty has been extolled and worshiped and kept just out of reach
for most of us. (Do you like having your picture taken? Do you like
seeing those pictures later? How do you feel when people ask you
your age? This issue of beauty runs deep!) For others, beauty has
been shamed, used, and abused. Some of you have learned that pos-
sessing beauty can be dangerous. And yet—and this is just astounding—*in spite* of all the pain and distress that beauty has caused us as
women, the desire remains.

During the midst of a talk I gave on the heart of a woman last
year, one of the women in the audience leaned over to a friend and
said, "I don't know what this whole thing is about—twirling skirts
and all." The words had barely left her mouth when she burst into
tears and had to leave the room. Little did she know how deep the
desire ran, and how much pain it had caused. Many of us have
hardened our hearts to this desire, the desire to be the Beauty. We,

too, have been hurt so deeply in this area that we no longer identify with, perhaps even resent, the longing. But it's there.

And it's *not* just the desire for an outward beauty, but more—a desire to be captivating in the depths of *who you are*. An external beauty without a depth of character is not true beauty at all. As the Proverb says, "Like a gold ring in a pig's snout is a beautiful woman who shows no discretion" (11:22). Cinderella is beautiful, yes, but she is also good. Her outward beauty would be hollow were it not for the beauty of her heart. That's why we love her. In *The Sound of Music*, the countess has Maria beat in the looks department, and they both know it. But Maria has a rare and beautiful depth of spirit. She has the capacity to love snowflakes on kittens and mean-spirited children. She sees the handiwork of God in music and laughter and climbing trees. Her soul is Alive. And we are drawn to her.

Ruth may have been a lovely, strong woman, but it is to her unrelenting courage and vulnerability and faith in God that Boaz is drawn. Esther is the most beautiful woman in the land, but it is her bravery and her cunning, good heart that moves the king to spare her people. This isn't about dresses and makeup. Beauty is so important that we'll come back to it again and again in this book. For now, don't you recognize that a woman yearns to be *seen*, and to be thought of as captivating? We desire to possess a beauty that is worth pursuing, worth fighting for, a beauty that is core to who we *truly* are. We want beauty that can be seen; beauty that can be felt; beauty that affects others; a beauty all our own to unveil.

THE HEART OF A MAN

As I (John here) described in *Wild at Heart*, there are three core desires in the heart of every man as well. (If you haven't read that book, you really should. It will open your eyes to the world of men.)

But they are uniquely masculine. For starters, every man wants a battle to fight. It's the whole thing with boys and weapons. Over the years our house has become an arsenal—pirate swords, Indian knives, light sabers, six-shooters, paintball markers, "air soft" guns (that name had to have been invented for moms). You name it. Our boys wrestled and hit and slammed one another up against the walls, and that is how they showed *affection*!

And look at the movies men love—*Braveheart, Gladiator, Top Gun, High Noon, Saving Private Ryan.* Men are made for battle. (And, ladies, don't you love the heroes of those movies? You might not want to fight in a war, but don't you long for a man who will fight for *you*? To have Daniel Day Lewis look you in the eyes and say, "No matter how long it takes, no matter how far, I will find you"?) Women don't fear a man's strength if he is a good man. In fact, *passivity* might make a man "safe," but it has done untold damage to women in the long run. It certainly did to Eve (more on that later).

Men also long for adventure. Boys love to climb and jump and see how fast they can ride their bikes (with no hands). Just look in your garage—all the gear and go-carts and motorcycles and ropes and boats and stuff. This isn't about "boys and their toys." Adventure is a deeply spiritual longing in the heart of every man. Adventure requires something of us, puts us to the test. Though we may fear the test, at the same time we yearn to be tested, to discover that we have what it takes.

Finally, every man longs for a Beauty to rescue. He really does. Where would Robin Hood be without Marian, or King Arthur without Guinevere? Lonely men fighting lonely battles. You see, it's not just that a man needs a battle to fight. He needs someone to fight *for*. There is nothing that inspires a man to courage so much as the woman he loves. Most of the daring (and okay, sometimes ridiculous) things young men do are to impress the girls. Men go to war carrying photos of their sweethearts in their wallets—that is a metaphor of this deeper longing, to fight for the Beauty. This is not to say that a woman is a "helpless creature" who can't live her life without a man. I'm saying that men long to offer their strength on behalf of a woman.

Now—can you see how the desires of a man's heart and the desires of a woman's heart were at least *meant* to fit beautifully together? A woman in the presence of a good man, a real man, loves being a woman. His strength allows her feminine heart to flourish. His pursuit draws out her beauty. And a man in the presence of a real woman loves being a man. Her beauty arouses him to play the man; it draws out his strength. She inspires him to be a hero. Would that we all were so fortunate.

By Way of the Heart

The longings God has written deep in your heart are telling you something essential about what it means to be a woman, and the life he meant for you to live. Now we know—many of those desires have gone unmet, or been assaulted, or simply so long neglected that most women end up living two lives. On the surface we are busy and efficient, professional, even. We are getting by. On the inside women lose themselves in a fantasy world or in cheap novels, or we give ourselves over to food or some other addiction to numb the ache of our hearts. But your heart is still there, crying out to be set free, to find the life your desires tell you of.

You can find that life—if you are willing to embark on a great adventure.

That is what we are inviting you to. Not to learn one more set of standards you fail to meet. Not toward a new set of rules to live by and things you ought to do. Something far, far better—a journey of the heart. A journey toward the restoration and release of the woman you always longed to be. This book is not about what you ought to do or who you ought to be. It's about discovering who you already are, as a woman. A woman who at her core was made for romance, made to play an irreplaceable role in a shared adventure, and who really does possess a beauty all her own to unveil. The woman God had in mind when he made Eve . . . and when he made *you*. Glorious, powerful, and captivating.

CHAPTER TWO

What Eve Alone Can Tell

❧

Even to see her walk across the room is a liberal education.
—C. S. LEWIS

Suddenly I turned around and she was standing there
With silver bracelets on her wrists and flowers in her hair
She walked up to me so gracefully and took my crown of thorns
Come in, she said I'll give you shelter from the storm.
—BOB DYLAN

*M*y parents named me after St. Anastasia, a woman martyred for her faith in the fifth century, so that every week during Mass, my name would be read aloud when certain saints were commemorated. That's why Stasi is spelled so weirdly. Take off the "Ana" at the beginning and the "a" at the end, and Stasi is what you get. I love it. And there's a deeper reason. I learned about Anastasia while in elementary school. Not St. Anastasia . . . but a princess. The youngest daughter of the last czar of Russia, Anastasia was rumored to have escaped the assassins who murdered the rest of her family. She was a young girl when her family was executed, and it was said that she was still alive, somewhere out there in the world, *incognito*. A true princess in disguise.

Women claimed to be her. One woman in particular was nearly

convincing. Still, Anastasia remained a mystery—a princess lost unto this world, hidden but true. I was intrigued and enamored by Princess Anastasia. I began to read everything I could get my hands on about Russian history. For a reason I could not explain, I felt a kinship with this mysterious princess, a connection to her. I wasn't pretending I was her, but still . . . something deep in my heart whispered that I, too, was more than met the eye. Perhaps I, too, was a part of royalty but my position had been lost. Perhaps I, too, was in disguise. My heart quickened at the thought of being a woman who was once a true princess.

I don't think I'm alone in this. Have you ever wondered why the Cinderella story keeps haunting us? Not only is it a perennial favorite of little girls; women love it too. Think of all the movies made along its themes, movies like *Pretty Woman, Ever After, A Cinderella Story, Maid in Manhattan,* and *Enchanted.* Why is this notion of a hidden princess (and a prince who comes to find her) so enduring? Is there something in our hearts that is trying to speak to us? Is it just fantasy, escapism? Or is there something more?

The desire of a woman's heart and the realities of a woman's life seem an ocean apart. Oh, we long for romance and an irreplaceable role in a great story; we long for beauty. But that's not the life we have. The result is a sense of shame. Having listened to the hearts of women for many, many years, both in the context of friendship and in the counseling office, we are struck by how deeply and universally women struggle with their self-worth. "I feel like a household appliance," one woman confessed to us. Now, this is not to say that men don't also wrestle with their sense of worth. But there is something deeper to this struggle for women, and far more universal. And there are reasons for it, reasons unique to Eve and her daughters.

We are reminded of Pascal's metaphor, that our unmet longings and unrequited desires are in fact "the miseries of a dethroned monarch." Mankind is like a king or queen in exile, and we cannot be happy until we have recovered our true state. What would you expect the Queen of a kingdom and the Beauty of the realm to feel when she wakes to find herself a laundress in a foreign land? A woman's struggle with her sense of worth points to something glorious she *was* designed to be. The great emptiness we feel points to the great place we *were* created for. It's true. All those legends and fairy tales of the undiscovered Princess and the Beauty hidden as a maid are more accurate than we thought. There's a *reason* little girls resonate with them so.

Rather than asking, "What should a woman do—what is her role?" it would be far more helpful to ask, "What *is* a woman—what is her design?" and, "Why did God place Woman in our midst?" We must go back to her beginnings, to the story of Eve. Even though we might have heard the story before (we have told it many times), it bears repeating. We clearly haven't learned its lessons—for if we had, men would treat women much, much differently, and women would view themselves in a far better light. So let us start there—with light. With the dawn of the world.

THE CROWN OF CREATION

To understand the creation story (John here), you must think of a work of art. Think of the Sistine Chapel, or the Venus de Milo, or Beethoven's Fifth, or of Sarah Brightman and Andre Bocelli singing "Time to Say Good-bye." Creation itself is a great work of art, and all works after it are echoes of the original. How it unfolded and where it reached its climax are mysteries worth unveiling. We will never truly understand women until we understand this. The scene begins in darkness,

> Darkness over the deep and God's breath hovering over the waters. (Gen. 1:2 *Alter*)

The breathless moment in the dark before the first notes of a great symphony or concert, a play, or an epic film. All is formless, empty, dark. Then a voice speaks.

Let there be light. (Gen. 1:3 *Alter*)

And suddenly, there is light, pure light, magnificent light. Its radiance will enable us to see now what is unfolding. The voice speaks again, and again.

Let there be a vault in the midst of the waters, and let it divide water from water. (Gen. 1:6 *Alter*)

Let the waters under the heavens be gathered in one place so that the dry land will appear. (Gen. 1:9 *Alter*)

Creation in its early stages begins like any great work of art—with uncut stone or a mass of clay, a rough sketch, a blank sheet of music. "Formless and empty" as Genesis 1:2 has it. Then God begins to fashion the raw materials he has made, like an artist working with the stone or sketch or page before him. Light and dark, heaven and earth, land and sea—it's beginning to take shape. With passion and brilliance the Creator works in large, sweeping movements on a grand scale. Great realms are distinguished from one another and established. Then he moves back over them again for a second pass as he begins to fill in color, detail, finer lines.

Let the earth grow grass, plants . . . and trees bearing fruit . . . (Gen. 1:11 *Alter*)

Let there be lights in the vault of the heavens . . . (Gen. 1:14 *Alter*)

> Let the waters swarm with the swarm of living creatures and let fowl fly over the earth. (Gen. 1:20 *Alter*)

Forest and meadow burst forth. Tulips and pine trees and moss-covered stones. And notice—the masterpiece is becoming more intricate, more intimate. He fills the night sky with a thousand million stars, and he *names* them, sets them in constellations. Into our world God opens his hand and the animals spring forth. Myriads of birds, in every shape and size and song, take wing—hawks, herons, pelicans. All the creatures of the sea leap into it—whales, dolphins, fish of a thousand colors and designs. Horses, gazelles, buffalo thunder across the plains, running like the wind. It is more astonishing than we could possibly imagine.

From water and stone, to pomegranate and rose, to leopard and nightingale, creation *ascends* in beauty. The plot is thickening; the symphony is building and swelling, higher and higher to a crescendo. No wonder "the morning stars sang together and all the angels shouted for joy" (Job 38:7). A great hurrah goes up from the heavens. The greatest of all masterpieces is emerging. What was once formless and empty is now overflowing with life and color and sound and movement in a thousand variations. Most importantly, notice that each creature is *more* intricate and noble and mysterious than the last. A cricket is amazing, but it cannot compare to a wild horse.

Then something truly astonishing takes place.

God sets his own image on the earth. He creates a being like himself. He creates a son.

> The LORD God formed the man from the dust of the ground and breathed into his nostrils the breath of life, and the man became a living being. (Gen. 2:7)

It is nearing the end of the sixth day, the end of the Creator's great labor, as Adam steps forth, the image of God, the triumph of his work. He alone is pronounced the son of God. Nothing in creation even comes close. Picture Michelangelo's *David*. He is . . . magnificent. Truly, the masterpiece seems complete. And yet, the Master says that something is not good, not right. Something is missing . . . and that something is Eve.

> And the Lord God cast a deep slumber on the human, and he
> slept, and He took one of his ribs and closed over the flesh where
> it had been, and the Lord God built the rib He had taken from
> the human into a woman and He brought her to the human.
> (Gen. 2:21–23 *Alter*)

She is the crescendo, the final, astonishing work of God. Woman. In one last flourish creation comes to a finish with *Eve*. She is the Master's finishing touch. How we wish this were an illustrated book, and we could show you now some painting or sculpture that captures this, like the stunning Greek sculpture of the goddess Nike of Samothrace, the winged beauty, just alighting on the prow of a great ship, her beautiful form revealed through the thin veils that sweep around her. Eve is . . . breathtaking.

Given the way creation unfolds, how it builds to ever higher and higher works of art, can there be any doubt that Eve is the crown of creation? As Paul later writes, man "is the image and glory of God; but the woman is the glory of man" (1 Cor. 11:7). Not an afterthought. Not a nice addition like an ornament on a tree. She is God's final touch, his *pièce de résistance*. She fills a place in the world nothing and no one else can fill. Step to a window, ladies, if you can. Better still, find some place with a view. Look out across the earth and say to yourselves, "The whole, vast world was incomplete without me. Creation reached its finishing touch in me."

WHAT DOES EVE SPEAK TO US?

The story of Eve holds such rich treasures for us to discover. The essence and purpose of a woman is unveiled here in the story of her creation. These profound, eternal, mythic themes are written not just here in the coming of Eve but in the soul of every woman after. Woman is the crown of creation—the most intricate, dazzling creature on earth. She has a crucial role to play, a destiny of her own.

And she, too, bears the image of God (Gen. 1:26), but in a way that only the feminine can speak. What can we learn from her? God wanted to reveal something about himself, so he gave us Eve. When you are with a woman, ask yourself, "What is she telling me about God?" It will open up wonders for you.

First, you'll discover that God is relational to his core, that he has a heart for romance. Second, that he longs to share adventures with us—adventures you cannot accomplish without him. And finally, that God has a beauty to unveil. A beauty that is captivating and powerfully redemptive.

ROMANCE AND RELATIONSHIPS: THE ANSWER TO LONELINESS

Man's love is of man's life a thing apart
'Tis a woman's whole existence.
—BYRON

Eve is created because things were not right without her. Something was not good. "It is not good for the man to be alone" (Gen. 2:18). This just staggers us. Think of it. The world is young and completely unstained. Adam is yet in his innocence and full of glory. He walks with God. Nothing stands between them. They share something none of us has ever known, only longed for: an unbroken friendship, untouched by sin. Yet something is not good? Something is missing? What could it possibly be? Eve. Woman. Femininity. Wow. Talk about significance.

To be specific, what was "not good" was the fact that the man was "alone." "It is not good for the human to be alone, I shall make him a sustainer beside him" (Gen. 2:18 *Alter*). How true this is. Whatever else we know about women, we know they are relational creatures to their cores. While little boys are killing one another in mock battles on the playground, little girls are negotiating relationships. If you want to know how people are doing, what's going on in our world, don't ask me—ask Stasi. I don't call friends and chat with them on the phone for an hour. I can't tell you who's dating whom, whose feelings have been hurt—ask Stasi.

This is so second nature, so assumed among women, that it goes unnoticed by them. They care more about relationships than just about anything else. Radio talk-show host Dennis Prager reports that when the topic of the day on his show is a "macro issue" like politics or finance, his callers will be Ed, Jack, Bill, and Dave. But when the topic is a "micro issue" involving human relationships, issues like dating or faithfulness or children, his callers will be Jane, Joanne, Susan, and Karen.

We were at a neighborhood Christmas party this past December. It's an annual thing, the only time the neighbors on our street get together. The men pretty quickly became a huddle in the kitchen (near the potato chips), engaged in a passionate debate about . . . concrete. I kid you not. That was our topic of the evening. Concrete driveways. Meanwhile, the women were in the living room talking about sex after menopause.

Most women *define* themselves in terms of their relationships, and the quality they deem those relationships to have. I am a mother, a sister, a daughter, a friend. Or I am alone. I'm not seeing anyone right now, or my children aren't calling, or my friends seem distant. This is not a weakness in women—it is a glory. A glory that reflects the heart of God.

GOD'S HEART FOR RELATIONSHIP

The vast desire and capacity a woman has for intimate relationships tells us of God's vast desire and capacity for intimate relationships. In fact, this may be *the* most important thing we ever learn about God—that he yearns for relationship with us. "Now this is eternal life: that they may know you, the only true God" (John 17:3). The whole story of the Bible is a love story between God and his people. He yearns for us. He *cares*. He has a tender heart.

> But Zion said, "The LORD has forsaken me, the Lord has forgotten me." "Can a mother forget the baby at her breast and have no compassion on the child she has borne? Though she may forget, I will not forget you!" . . . declares the LORD. (Isa. 49:14–15, 18)

> I will give them a heart to know me, that I am the LORD. They will be my people, and I will be their God, for they will return to me with all their heart. (Jer. 24:7)

> O Jerusalem, Jerusalem . . . how often I have longed to gather your children together, as a hen gathers her chicks under her wings, but you were not willing. (Matt. 23:37)

What a comfort to know that this universe we live in is relational at its core, that our God is a tenderhearted God who yearns for relationship with us. If you have any doubt about that, simply look at the message he sent us in Woman. Amazing. Not only does God long *for* us, but he longs to be loved *by* us. Oh, how we've missed this. How many of you see God as longing to be loved by you? We see him as strong and powerful, but not as needing us, vulnerable to us, yearning to be desired. But as I wrote in *Wild at Heart*,

> After years of hearing the heart-cry of women, I am convinced beyond a doubt of this: God wants to be loved. He wants to be a priority to someone. How could we have missed this? From cover to cover, from beginning to end, the cry of God's heart is, "Why won't you choose me?" It is amazing to me how humble, how vulnerable God is on this point. "You will find me," says the Lord, "when you seek me with all your heart" (Jer. 29:13). In other words, "Look for me, pursue me—I want you to pursue me." Amazing. As Tozer says, "God waits to be wanted."

Can there be any doubt that God wants to be sought after? The first and greatest of all commands is to love him (Mark 12:29–30; Matt. 22:36–38). He *wants* us to love him. To seek him with all our hearts. A woman longs to be sought after, too, with the whole heart of her pursuer. God longs to be *desired*. Just as a woman longs to be desired. This is not some weakness or insecurity on the part of a woman, that deep yearning to be desired. "Take me for longing," Alison Krauss sings, "or leave me behind." God feels the same way. Remember the story of Martha and Mary? Mary chose God, and Jesus said that *that* is what he wanted. "Mary has chosen what is better" (Luke 10:42). She chose me.

Life changes dramatically when romance comes into our lives. Christianity changes dramatically when we discover that it, too, is a great romance. That God yearns to share a life of beauty, intimacy, and adventure with us. "I have loved you with an everlasting love" (Jer. 31:3). This whole world was made for romance—the rivers and the glens, the meadows and beaches. Flowers, music, a kiss. But we have a way of forgetting all that, losing ourselves in work and worry. Eve—God's message to the world in feminine form—invites us to romance. Through her, God makes romance a priority of the universe.

So God endows Woman with certain qualities that are essential to relationship, qualities that speak of God. She is inviting. She is vulnerable. She is tender. She embodies mercy. She is also fierce and fiercely devoted. As the old saying goes, "Hell hath no fury like a woman scorned." That's just how God acts when he isn't chosen. "I, the LORD your God, am a jealous God who will not share your affection with any other god!" (Ex. 20:5 NLT). A woman's righteous jealousy speaks of the jealousy of God for us.

Tender and inviting, intimate and alluring, fiercely devoted. Oh yes, our God has a passionate, romantic heart. Just look at Eve.

AN ADVENTURE TO SHARE

While Eve has a glory for relationship, that is *not* all she is essential for. Back in Genesis, when God sets his image bearers on the earth, he gives them their mission:

> And God said, "Let us make a human in our image, by our likeness, to hold sway over the fish of the sea and the fowl of the heavens and the cattle and the wild beasts and all the crawling things that crawl upon the earth.
>
> And God created the human in his image,
> in the image of God He created him,
> male and female He created them.
>
> And God blessed them, and God said to them, "Be fruitful and multiply and fill the earth and conquer it, and hold sway over the fish of the sea and the fowl of the heavens and every beast that crawls upon the earth." (Gen. 1:26–28 *Alter*)

Call it the Human Mission—to be all and do all God sent us here to do. And notice—the mission to be fruitful and conquer and hold sway is given *both* to Adam *and* to Eve. "And God said to *them* . . ." Eve is standing right there when God gives the world over to us. She has a vital role to play; she is a partner in this great adventure. All that human beings were intended to do here on earth—all the creativity and exploration, all the battle and rescue and nurture—we were intended to do *together*. In fact, not only is Eve needed, but she is *desperately* needed.

When God creates Eve, he calls her an *ezer kenegdo*. "It is not good for the man to be alone, I shall make him [an *ezer kenegdo*]" (Gen. 2:18 *Alter*). Hebrew scholar Robert Alter, who has spent years translating the book of Genesis, says that this phrase is "notoriously difficult to translate." The various attempts we have in English are "helper" or "companion" or the notorious "help meet." Why are these translations so incredibly wimpy, boring, flat . . . disappointing? What is a help meet, anyway? What little girl dances through the house singing, "One day I shall be a help meet"? Companion? A dog can be a companion. Helper? Sounds like Hamburger Helper. Alter is getting close when he translates it "sustainer beside him."

The word *ezer* is used only twenty other places in the entire Old Testament. And in every other instance the person being described is God himself, when you need him to come through for you *desperately*.

There is no one like the God of Jeshurun, who rides on the heavens to help you . . .

Blessed are you, O Israel! Who is like you, a people saved by the LORD? He is your shield and *helper* and your glorious sword. (Deut. 33:26, 29, emphasis added)

I lift up my eyes to the hills—where does my help come from?
My *help* comes from the LORD, the Maker of heaven and earth.
(Ps. 121:1–2, emphasis added)

May the LORD answer you when you are in distress; may the
name of the God of Jacob protect you. May he send you *help*. (Ps.
20:1–2, emphasis added)

We wait in hope for the LORD; he is our *help* and our shield. (Ps.
33:20, emphasis added)

O house of Israel, trust in the LORD—he is their *help* and shield.
O house of Aaron, trust in the LORD—he is their *help* and shield.
You who fear him, trust in the LORD—he is their *help* and shield.
(Ps. 115:9–11, emphasis added)

Most of the contexts are life and death, by the way, and God is
your only hope. Your *ezer*. If he is not there beside you . . . you are
dead. A better translation therefore of *ezer* would be "lifesaver."
Kenegdo means alongside, or opposite to, a counterpart.

You see, the life God calls us to is not a safe life. Ask Joseph,
Abraham, Moses, Deborah, Esther—any of the friends of God from
the Old Testament. Ask Mary and Lazarus; ask Peter, James, and
John; ask Priscilla and Aquila—any of the friends of God in the
New Testament. God calls us to a life involving frequent risks and
many dangers. Why else would we need him to be our *ezer*? You
don't need a lifesaver if your mission is to be a couch potato. You
need an *ezer* when your life is in constant danger.

Picture the character Arwen in the mythic motion-picture
trilogy *The Lord of the Rings*. Arwen is a princess, a beautiful and
brave elf maiden. She comes into the story in the nick of time to
rescue the little hobbit Frodo just as the poisoned wound moving
toward his heart is about to claim him.

ARWEN: He's fading. He's not going to last. We must get him to my
father. I've been looking for you for two days. There are five
wraiths behind you. Where the other four are, I do not know.

ARAGORN: Stay with the hobbits. I'll send horses for you.

ARWEN: I'm the faster rider. I'll take him.

ARAGORN: The road is too dangerous.

ARWEN: I do not fear them.

ARAGORN: (*Relinquishing to her, he takes her hand.*) Arwen, ride hard.
Don't look back.

It is she, not the warrior Aragorn, who rides with glory and
speed. She is Frodo's only hope. She is the one entrusted with his life
and with him, the future of all Middle Earth. She is his *ezer kenegdo*.

That longing in the heart of a woman to share life together as
a great adventure—that comes straight from the heart of God, who
also longs for this. He does not want to be an option in our lives.
He does not want to be an appendage, a tagalong. Neither does any
woman. God is essential. He wants us to need him—desperately.
Eve is essential. She has an irreplaceable role to play. And so you'll
see that women are endowed with fierce devotion, an ability to suffer great hardships, a vision to make the world a better place.

BEAUTY TO UNVEIL

Beauty.

I (John) just let out a deep sigh. That we even need to explain
how beauty is so *absolutely essential* to God only shows how dull we

have grown to him, to the world in which we live, and to Eve. Far too many years of our own spiritual lives were lived with barely a nod to beauty, to the central role that beauty plays in the life of God and in our own lives. We held to the importance of truth and goodness. Had you suggested beauty to us, we might have nodded, but not really understood. How could we have missed this?

Beauty is essential to God. No—that's not putting it strongly enough. Beauty is the essence of God.

The first way we know this is through nature, the world God has given us. Scripture says that the created world is filled with the glory of God (Isa. 6:3). In what way? Primarily through its *beauty*. We had a wet spring here in Colorado, and the wildflowers are coming up everywhere—lupine and wild iris and Shasta daisies and a dozen others. The aspens have their heart-shaped leaves again, trembling in the slightest breeze. Massive thunderclouds are rolling in, bringing with them the glorious sunsets they magnify. The earth in summer is brimming with beauty, beauty of such magnificence and variety and unembarrassed lavishness, ripe beauty, lush beauty, beauty given to us with such generosity and abundance it is almost scandalous.

Nature is not primarily functional. It is primarily beautiful. Stop for a moment and let that sink in. We're so used to evaluating everything (and everyone) by their usefulness that this thought will take a minute or two to begin to dawn on us. Nature is not primarily functional. It is primarily *beautiful*. Which is to say, beauty is in and of itself a great and glorious good, something we need in large and daily doses (for our God has seen fit to arrange for this). Nature at the height of its glory shouts, *Beauty is Essential!* revealing that Beauty is the essence of God. The whole world is full of his glory.

Next, there are the visions given to John, who was taken in the Spirit to behold God. As we can only imagine, he finds it hard to put into words what he saw (he keeps using the word *like*, as if grasping to find any comparison that might help us appreciate what he beheld).

> The one sitting on the throne was as brilliant as gemstones—jasper and carnelian. And the glow of an emerald circled his throne like a rainbow . . . In front of the throne was a shiny sea of glass, sparkling like crystal. (Rev. 4:3, 6 NLT)

Is there any doubt that the God John beheld was beautiful *beyond* description? But of course. God must be even more glorious than this glorious creation, for it "foretells" or "displays" the glory that is God's. John describes God as radiant as gemstones, as richly adorned in golds and reds and greens and blues, shimmering as crystal. Why, these are the very things that Cinderella is given—the very things women still prefer to adorn themselves with when they want to look their finest. Hmmm. And isn't that just what a woman longs to hear? "You are radiant this evening. You are absolutely breathtaking."

Saints from ages past would speak of the highest pleasures of heaven as simply beholding the beauty of God, the "beatific vision."

> The reason a woman wants a beauty to unveil, the reason she asks, *Do you delight in me?* is simply that God does as well. God is captivating beauty. As David prays, "One thing I ask of the LORD, this is what I seek: that I may . . . gaze upon the beauty of the LORD" (Ps. 27:4). Can there be any doubt that God wants to be *worshiped*? That He wants to be seen, and for us to be captivated by what we see? (*Wild at Heart*)

But in order to make the matter perfectly clear, God has given us Eve. The crowning touch of creation. Beauty is the essence of a woman. We want to be perfectly clear that we mean *both* a physical beauty and a soulful/spiritual beauty. The one depends upon and flows out of the other. Yes, the world cheapens and prostitutes beauty, making it all about a perfect figure few women can attain. But Christians minimize it too, or overspiritualize it, making it all about "character." We must recover the prize of Beauty. The church must take it back. Beauty is too vital to lose.

God gave Eve a beautiful form *and* a beautiful spirit. She expresses beauty in both. Better, she expresses beauty simply in who she is. Like God, it is her *essence*.

Stasi and I just spent a weekend together in Santa Fe, New Mexico, which boasts the third largest gathering of art galleries in the world. We love to wander for hours through those galleries and gardens, looking for those works of art that particularly capture us. Toward the afternoon of our second day, Stasi asked me, "Have you seen one painting of a naked man?" The point was startling. After days of looking at maybe a thousand pieces of art, we had not seen one painting devoted to the beauty of the naked masculine form. Not one. (Granted, there are a few examples down through history . . . but only a few.) However, the beauty of Woman was celebrated everywhere, hundreds of times over in paintings and sculptures. There is a reason for this.

For one thing, men look ridiculous lying on a bed buck naked, half-covered with a sheet. It doesn't fit the essence of masculinity. Something in you wants to say, "Get up already and get a job. Cut the grass. Get to work." For Adam is captured best in motion, *doing* something. His essence is *strength in action*. That is what he speaks to the world. He bears the image of God, who is a warrior. On behalf of God, Adam says, "God will come through. God is on the move." That is why a passive man is so disturbing. His passivity defies his very essence. It violates the way he bears God's image. A passive man says, "God will not come through. He is not acting on your behalf."

On the other hand, and bear with us a moment, Eve just doesn't look right in a scene of brutal combat, or chopping a tree down. From time immemorial, when artists have tried to capture the essence of Eve, they have painted her (or photographed her, or sculpted her) *at rest.* There is no agenda here, no social stigmatizing or cultural pressure. This is true across all cultures and down through time. What have the artists seen that we have not? Eve speaks something differently to the world than Adam does. Through her beauty.

Why Beauty Matters

Every experience of beauty points to [eternity].
—Hans Urs von Balthasar

Beauty is powerful. It may be the most powerful thing on earth. It is dangerous. Because it *matters.* Let us try and explain why.

First, beauty *speaks.* Oxford bishop Richard Harries wrote, "It is the beauty of the created order which gives an answer to our questionings about God." And we do have questions, don't we? Questions born out of our disappointments, our sufferings, our fears. Augustine said he found answers to his questions in the beauty of the world.

> I said to all these things, "Tell me of my God who you are not, tell me something about him." And with a great voice they cried out: "He made us" (Ps. 99:3). My question was the attention I gave to them, and their response was their beauty.

And what does beauty say to us? Think of what it is like to be caught in traffic for more than an hour. Horns blaring, people shouting obscenities. Exhaust pouring in your windows, suffocating you. Then remember what it's like to come into a beautiful place, a garden or a meadow or a quiet beach. There is room for your soul. It expands. You can breathe again. You can rest. It is good. All is well. I sit outside on a summer evening and just listen and behold and drink it all in, and my heart begins to quiet and peace begins to come into my soul. My heart tells me, *All will be well,* as Julian of Norwich concluded. "And all manner of things will be well."

That is what beauty says, *All shall be well.*

And this is what it's like to be with a woman at rest, a woman comfortable in her feminine beauty. She is enjoyable to be with. She is lovely. In her presence your heart stops holding its breath. You relax and believe once again that all will be well. And this is also why a woman who is striving is so disturbing, for a woman who is not at rest in her heart says to the world, *All is not well. Things are not going to turn out all right.* "Like a fountain troubled," as Shakespeare said, "muddy, ill-seeming, thick, bereft of beauty." We *need* what Beauty speaks. What it says is hard to put into words. But part of its message is that all is well. All will be well.

Beauty also *invites.* Recall what it is like to hear a truly beautiful piece of music. It captures you; you want to sit down and just drink it in. We buy the CD and play it many times over. (This is not visual, showing us that beauty is deeper than looks.) Music like this commands your attention, invites you to come more deeply into it. The same is true of a beautiful garden, or a scene in nature. You want to enter in, explore, partake of it, feast upon it. We describe a great book as "captivating." It draws you in, holds your attention. You can't wait to get back to it, spend time with it. All of the responses that God wants of us. All of the responses a woman wants too. Beauty invites.

Beauty *nourishes.* It is a kind of food our souls crave. A woman's breast is among the loveliest of all God's works, and it is with her breast that she nourishes a baby—a stunning picture of the way in which Beauty itself nourishes us. In fact, a woman's body is one of the most beautiful of all God's creations. "Too much of eternity," as William Blake said, "for the eye of man." It nourishes, offers life. That is such a profound metaphor for Beauty itself. As C. S. Lewis said,

> We do not want merely to see beauty, though, God knows, even that is bounty enough. We want something else which can hardly be put into words—to be united with the beauty we see, to pass into it, to receive it into ourselves. (*The Weight of Glory*)

Beauty *comforts*. There is something profoundly healing about it. Have you ever wondered why we send flowers to the bereaved? In the midst of their suffering and loss, only a gift of beauty says enough or says it right. After I lost my dearest friend, Brent, there were months when only beauty helped. I could not hear words of counsel. I could not read or even pray. Only beauty helped. There's a touching story told from the hospitals of WWII, where a young and badly wounded soldier was brought in from a hellish week of fighting. After doing what she could for him, the nurse asked if there was anything else she could do. "Yes," he said. "Could you just put on some lipstick while I watch?" Beauty comforts. It soothes the soul.

Beauty *inspires*. After beholding all the marvelous wonders of the creation of Narnia (as told in *The Magician's Nephew* by C. S. Lewis), the cabbie says, "Glory be! I'd have been a better man all my life if I'd known there were things like this!" Or as Jack Nicholson says to Helen Hunt at the end of *As Good As It Gets*, "You make me want to be a better man." Isn't it true? Think of what it might have been like to have been in the presence of a woman like Mother Teresa. Her life was so beautiful, and it called us to something higher. A teacher in the inner city explained to us why he insisted on putting a fountain and flowers in the courtyard of the building. "Because these children need to be inspired. They need to know that life can be better." Beauty inspires.

Beauty is *transcendent*. It is our most immediate experience of the eternal. Think of what it's like to behold a gorgeous sunset or the ocean at dawn. Remember the ending of a great story. We yearn to linger, to experience it all our days. Sometimes the beauty is so deep it pierces us with longing. For what? For life as it was meant to be. Beauty reminds us of an Eden we have never known, but somehow know our hearts were created for. Beauty speaks of heaven to come, when all shall be beautiful. It haunts us with eternity. Beauty says, *There is a glory calling to you.* And if there is a glory, there is a source of glory. What great goodness could have possibly created this? What generosity gave us this to behold? Beauty draws us to God.

All these things are true for any experience of Beauty. But they are *especially* true when we experience the beauty of a woman—her eyes, her form, her voice, her heart, her spirit, her life. She speaks all of this far more profoundly than anything else in all creation, because she is *incarnate*; she is personal. It flows to us from an immortal being. She is beauty through and through. "For where is any author in the world Teaches such beauty as a woman's eye?" (Shakespeare).

Beauty is, without question, the most *essential* and the most *misunderstood* of all of God's qualities—of all feminine qualities too. We know it has caused untold pain in the lives of women. But even there something is speaking. Why so much heartache over beauty? We don't ache over being geniuses or fabulous hockey players. Women ache over the issue of beauty—they ache to be beautiful, to believe they are beautiful, and they worry over keeping it if ever they can find it. I was just at Starbucks and overheard the conversation between two women in their late fifties sitting at the table next to mine. The subject? Weight and diets. Their struggle with the issue of beauty.

A woman knows, down in her soul, that she longs to bring beauty to the world. She might be mistaken on how (something every woman struggles with), but she longs for a beauty to unveil.

This is not just culture, or the need to "get a man." This is in her heart, part of her design.

BUT WHY A BEAUTY TO UNVEIL?

One of the deepest ways a woman bears the image of God is in her mystery. By "mystery" we don't mean "forever beyond your knowing," but "something to be explored." "It is the glory of God to conceal a matter," says the book of Proverbs, "to search out a matter is the glory of kings" (25:2). God yearns to be known. But he wants to be *sought after* by those who would know him. He says, "You will seek me and find me when you seek me with all your heart" (Jer. 29:13). There is dignity here; God does not throw himself at any passerby. He is no harlot. If you would know him you must love him; you must seek him with your whole heart. This is crucial to any woman's soul, not to mention her sexuality. "You cannot simply have me. You must seek me, pursue me. I won't let you in unless I know you love me."

Is not the Trinity a great mystery? Not something to be solved, but known with ever-deepening pleasure and awe, something to be enjoyed. Just like God, a woman is not a problem to be solved but a vast wonder to be enjoyed. This is so true of her sexuality. Few women can or even want to "just do it." Foreplay is crucial to her heart, the whispering and loving and exploring of one another that culminates in intercourse. That is a picture of what it means to love her *soul*. She yearns to be known and that takes time and intimacy. It requires an unveiling. As she is sought after, she reveals more of her beauty. As she unveils her beauty, she draws us to know her more deeply.

Whatever else it means to be feminine, it is depth and mystery and complexity, with beauty as its very essence. Now, lest despair set in, let us say as clearly as we can:

Every woman has a beauty to unveil.

Every woman.

Because she bears the image of God. She doesn't have to conjure it, go get it from a salon, have plastic surgery or breast implants. No, beauty is an *essence* that is given to every woman at her creation.

IN CLOSING

It is very important for you to pause just now and ask yourself, "What did I hear them say?"

We did not say that a woman is prized only for her good looks. We did not say a woman is here merely to complete a man, and therefore a single woman is somehow missing her destiny. What we said was, first, that Eve is the crown of creation. There is something uniquely magnificent and powerful about a woman. We tried to reveal the immeasurable dignity, the holiness of your feminine heart by showing that it is *God* who longs for Romance; it is *God* who longs to be our *ezer*; it is *God* who reveals beauty as essential to life. You are the image bearer of this God. That is why you long for those things too.

There is a radiance hidden in your heart that the world desperately needs.

CHAPTER THREE

Haunted by a Question

❦

> *She knew treachery,*
> *Rapine, deceit and lust, and ills enow*
> *To be a woman.*
> —JOHN DONNE

> *O most pernicious woman!*
> —WILLIAM SHAKESPEARE

*I*was standing in line at the grocery store buying a few last-minute items when I heard her. "*That* is the fifteen-item-or-*less* line, ma'am," she hissed. I looked around wondering who the woman was talking about. My own cart had the required fifteen items. I knew it. I had counted them twice to be sure. When she motioned for her husband to look at the wicked infidel, I saw that she was directing her comments at me! Glancing back I told her that I only had the prescribed fifteen items in my cart. She rolled away in an angry huff.

Soon, she was back in the line next to mine with her husband following. She muttered loudly, accusingly, her voice filled with sarcasm, "She *says* she only has *fifteen* items." At this point, to say I became defensive is a massive understatement. Rage welled up inside me. I felt hot, surprising myself at the intensity of my reaction. Leaning around the candy bars I spoke angrily to her, "I do only have fifteen items, ma'am. Do you want to come over here and *count* them?" Her husband held up his hand signaling me to back off, let it go.

Embarrassed, I quieted and then paid for my order—vindicated that there were indeed only fifteen items in my cart. Oh, how I wanted to show her my receipt. Driving home, still upset, I had to pull over. I mean, I was shaking. I had just gotten into a "fight" with a stranger in the grocery store over the fifteen-item-or-less line. What was going on? What was *that* about?

EVE—WHAT HAPPENED?

Eve was given to the world as the incarnation of a beautiful, captivating God—a life-offering, life-saving lover, a relational specialist, full of tender mercy and hope. Yes, she brought a strength to the world, but not a striving, sharp-edged strength. She was inviting, alluring, captivating.

Is that how you experience the women you know? Is that how people experience you?

Why do so few women have anything close to a life of romance? Loneliness and emptiness are far more common themes—so entirely common that most women buried their longings for romance long ago and are now living merely to survive, get through the week. And it's not just romance—why are most of the relationships of women fraught with hardship? Their friendships, their families, their best friends all seem to have come down with a sort of virus that makes them fundamentally unavailable, leaving a woman lonely at the end of the day. Even when relationships are good, it's never enough. Where does this bottomless pit in us come from?

And women are tired. We are drained. But it's not from a life of shared adventures. No, the weariness of women comes from lives that are crammed with routine, with chores, with hundreds of demands. As Chekov said, "Any idiot can face a crisis. It's the day to day living that wears you out." Somehow, somewhere between our youth and yesterday, *efficiency* has taken the place of adventure. Most women do not feel they are playing an irreplaceable role in a great Story. Oh no. We struggle to know if we matter at all. If we are at home, we feel ashamed we don't have a "real life" in the outside world. We are swallowed by laundry. If we have a career, we feel as though we are missing out on more important matters like marriage and children. We are swallowed by meetings.

A WOMAN'S DEEPEST QUESTION

Finally, most women doubt very much that they have any genuine beauty to unveil. It is, in fact, our deepest doubt. When it comes to the issues surrounding beauty, we vacillate between striving and resignation. New diets, new outfits, new hair color. Work out; work on your life; try this discipline or that new program for self-improvement. Oh, forget it. Who cares anyway? Put up a shield and get on with life. Hide. Hide in busyness; hide in church activities; hide in depression. There is nothing captivating about me. Certainly not *inside* me. I'll be lucky to pull it off on the outside.

When I'm going out to a party or gathering, or just to dinner at a friend's house—really, anywhere I am meeting other people—I feel nervous. Often I'm not aware of what I'm truly feeling, but I find myself reapplying lipstick in the car on the way. The more nervous I feel, the more lipstick goes on. Getting close to the destination, I reapply more lipstick. A little closer, on goes some more. Turning into their street, on goes another layer of Sunset Rose or whatever. I clued into this "habit" some time ago when I caught myself putting on another unnecessary layer. What was I doing? *I was afraid.* At least if my makeup looks good, something deep inside me reasoned, maybe I won't be exposed. Found out. Seen.

Every woman is haunted by Eve in the core of her being. She knows, if only when she passes a mirror, that she is not what she was meant to be. We are more keenly aware of our own shortcomings than anyone else. Remembering the glory that was once ours awakens my heart to an ache that has long gone unfulfilled. It's almost too much to hope for, too much to have lost.

You see, every little girl—and every little boy—shares a fundamental longing to be loved. But oftentimes, the way this need plays out is very different. Each child born into this broken world is asking one fundamental question. But they are very different questions, depending on whether you are a little boy or a little girl. Little boys want to know, *Do I have what it takes?* All that rough and tumble, all that daring and superhero dress up, all of that is a boy seeking to prove that he does have what it takes. He was made in the image of a warrior God. Nearly all a man does is fueled by his search for validation, that longing he carries for an answer to his Question.

Little girls want to know, *Am I lovely?* The twirling skirts, the dress up, the longing to be pretty and to be seen—that is what that's all about. We are seeking an answer to our Question. When I was a girl of maybe five years old, I remember standing on top of the coffee table in my grandparents' living room and singing my heart out. I wanted to capture attention—especially my father's attention. I wanted to be captivating. We all did. But for most of us, the answer to our Question when we were young was, "No, there is nothing captivating about you. Get off the coffee table." Nearly all a woman does in her adult life is fueled by her longing to be delighted in, her longing to be beautiful, to be irreplaceable, to have her Question answered, "Yes!"

Why does the Question linger so? Why haven't we been able to find and rest in a wonderful, personal answer for our own hearts?

THE FALL OF EVE

When the world was young and we were innocent—both man and woman—we were naked and unashamed (Gen. 2:25). Nothing to hide. Simply . . . glorious. And while that world was young, and we, too, were young and beautiful and full of life, a corner was turned. Something happened, which we have heard about, but never fully understood, or we would see it playing itself out every day of our lives, and, more important, we would *also* see the chances given to us every day to reverse what happened.

> Now the serpent was the shrewdest of all the creatures the LORD God had made. "Really?" he asked the woman. "Did God really say you must not eat any of the fruit in the garden?"
>
> "Of course we may eat it," the woman told him. "It's only the fruit from the tree at the center of the garden that we are not allowed to eat. God says we must not eat it or even touch it, or we will die."
>
> "You won't die!" the serpent hissed. "God knows that your eyes will be opened when you eat it. You will become just like God, knowing everything, both good and evil."
>
> The woman was convinced. The fruit looked so fresh and delicious, and it would make her so wise! So she ate some of the fruit. She also gave some to her husband, who was with her. Then he ate it, too. (Gen. 3:1–6 NLT)

Alas.

There are no words.

Wail; beat your chest; fall to your knees; let out a long, lonesome howl of bitter remorse.

The woman was convinced. That's it? Just like that? In a matter of moments? Convinced of what? Look in your own heart—you'll see. Convinced that God was holding out on her. Convinced that she could not trust his heart toward her. Convinced that in order to have the best possible life, she must take matters into her own hands. And so she did. She is the first to fall. In disobeying God she also violated her very essence. Eve is supposed to be Adam's *ezer kenegdo*, like one who comes to *save*. She is to bring him life, invite him to life. Instead, she invited him to his death.

Now, to be fair, Adam doesn't exactly ride to her rescue.

Let me ask you a question: Where is Adam, while the serpent is tempting Eve? He's standing right there: "She also gave some to her husband, who was with her, and he ate it" (3:6). The Hebrew for "with her" means right there, elbow to elbow. Adam isn't away in another part of the forest; he has no alibi. He is standing right there, watching the whole thing unravel. What does he do? Nothing. Absolutely nothing. He says not a word, doesn't lift a finger. [I'm indebted to Crabb, Hudson, and Andrews for pointing this out in *The Silence of Adam*.] He won't risk, he won't fight, and he won't rescue Eve. Our first father—the first real man—gave in to paralysis. He denied his very nature and went passive. And every man after him, every son of Adam, carries in his heart now the same failure. Every man repeats the sin of Adam, every day. We won't risk, we won't fight, and we won't rescue Eve. We truly are a chip off the old block. (*Wild at Heart*)

You can see this play itself out every day. Men, just when we need them to come through for us . . . check out. They disappear, go silent and passive. "He won't talk to me," is many a woman's lament. They won't fight for us.

And women? We tend to be grasping, reaching, controlling. We are often enchanted, like Eve, so easily falling prey to the lies of our Enemy. Having forfeited our confidence in God, we believe that in order to have the life we want, we must take matters into our own hands. And we ache with an emptiness nothing seems able to fill.

THE CURSE

To the woman he said,

"I will greatly increase your pains in childbearing;
with pain you will give birth to children.
Your desire will be for your husband,
and he will rule over you."

To Adam he said, "Because you listened to your wife and ate from the tree about which I commanded you, 'You must not eat of it,'

"Cursed is the ground because of you;
through painful toil you will eat of it
all the days of your life.
It will produce thorns and thistles for you." (Gen. 3:16–18)

Now, it would be good for us to give careful attention to all that has unfolded here—especially the curses God pronounced—for the story explains our lives today, east of Eden. For one thing, the curse on Adam cannot be limited *only* to actual thorns and thistles. If that were so, then every man who chooses not to be a farmer gets to escape the curse. Take a white-collar job and you're scot-free. No, the meaning is deeper and the implications are for every son of Adam. Man is cursed with *futility* and *failure*. Life is going to be hard for a man now in the place he will feel it most. Failure is a man's worst fear.

In just the same way, the curse for Eve and all her daughters cannot be limited *only* to babies and marriage, for if that were true then every single woman without children gets to escape the curse. Not so. The meaning is deeper and the implications are for *every* daughter of Eve. Woman is cursed with loneliness (relational heartache), with the urge to control (especially her man), and with the dominance of men (which is not how things were meant to be, and we are not saying it is a good thing—it is the fruit of the Fall and a sad fact of history). [I am also indebted to Dan Allender who first pointed out these insights to me.]

Isn't it true? Aren't your deepest worries and heartaches relational—aren't they connected to some*one*? Even when things are good, is your vast capacity for intimacy ever filled in a lasting way? There *is* an emptiness in us that we continually try to feed. And can't you see how much you need to have things under your control— whether it's a project or a ministry or a marriage? Are you comfortable trusting your well-being to someone else? And haven't you felt "this is a man's world," felt your vulnerability as a woman to be a liability? Most women hate their vulnerability. We are not inviting— we are *guarded.* Most of our energy is spent trying to hide our true selves and control our worlds to have some sense of security.

When a man goes bad, as every man has in some way gone bad after the Fall, what is most deeply marred is his strength. He either becomes a passive, weak man—strength surrendered—or he becomes a violent, driven man—strength unglued. When a woman falls from grace, what is most deeply marred is her tender vulnerability, beauty that invites to life. She becomes a dominating, controlling woman—or a desolate, needy, mousy woman. Or some odd combination of both, depending on her circumstances.

Dominating Women

Think for a moment about the characters of women you dislike— even despise—in movies. (That seems a more charitable place to start—they are, after all, fictional characters.) In *The Horse Whisperer*, Annie MacLean (played by Kristin Scott Thomas) is a sharp, sophisticated New York professional, the editor of a leading women's magazine. She is also an incredibly controlling woman. Annie's daughter is hospitalized in critical condition following a riding accident that takes the life of her best friend, claims her leg, and terribly injures her horse. Understandably, Annie is shaken to the core. The way she handles her crisis is to dominate—the doctors, the nurses, her husband, even her maimed daughter. At one point she notices her daughter's IV bag is running low.

> "You can't leave it to these people."
> (*She steps into the hall, apprehends the first nurse coming by.*)
> "Excuse me—my daughter needs a new IV."
> "Yes, I know—we have her down . . ."
> "Well I'd like you to take care of it now please."
> (*"Please" is a barely veiled threat, more like, "or else." Annie walks back into the room and explains to her embarrassed husband.*)
> "You have to stay on top of these people constantly."

She needs no one. She is in charge—"on top of things constantly." She is a woman who knows how to get what she wants. (Some of us might even admire that!) But consider this—there is nothing merciful about her, nothing tender, and certainly nothing vulnerable. She has forsaken essential aspects of her femininity.

There is the despicable Mrs. John Dashwood in *Sense and Sensibility*. John Dashwood's father dies at the beginning of the story, leaving his wife and three daughters to the care of his only son, to whom he has bequeathed his entire estate. But with his dying breath he has commanded that the women be financially provided for through the good will of his son. During the carriage ride home from the funeral, Mrs. Dashwood—the conniving and greedy sister-in-law—spins a web of manipulation around her husband, John, and by the time the ride is over, both mother and sisters are penniless.

Think of Tom Cruise's fiancée at the opening of *Jerry Maguire* (the one who decks him). "I'm not going to let you do this to me, Jerry." Or Rose's mother in *Titanic*. "We have to survive." That line is also said by the horrid mother in *Strictly Ballroom*. And all those villains like Cruella de Ville and Esmeralda ("mirror, mirror on the wall"). Notice also that most of the wicked witches are women. Or stepmothers. Have you ever wondered why it was that for years—until the feminist movement, it might be noted with irony—hurricanes were named after women? Now, sure, a calculating, heartless man makes a frightening villain. But somehow it's even worse when the villain is a woman.

Fallen Eve controls her relationships. She *refuses* to be vulnerable. And if she cannot secure her relationships, then she kills her heart's longing for intimacy so that she will be safe and in control. She becomes a woman "who doesn't need anyone—especially a man." How this plays out over the course of her life and how the wounds of her childhood shape her heart's convictions are often a complex story, one worth knowing. But beneath it all, behind it all, is a simple truth: women dominate and control because they fear their vulnerability. Far from God and far from Eden, it seems a perfectly reasonable way to live. But consider also this: "Whatever is not from faith is sin" (Rom. 14:23 NKJV). That self-protective way of relating to others has nothing to do with real loving, and nothing to do with deeply trusting God. It is our gut-level response to a dangerous world.

Now, this is not to say a woman can't be strong. What we are saying is that far too many women forfeit their femininity in order to feel safe and in control. Their strength feels more masculine than feminine. There is nothing inviting or alluring, nothing tender or merciful about them. The archetype would be the infamous Lady Macbeth, who asks the gods to "unsex her," remove her femininity, so that she can control the fate of the man in her life, and thus secure her own fate.

Controlling women are those of us who don't trust anyone else to drive our cars. Or help in our kitchens. Or speak at our retreats or our meetings. Or carry something for us. Make a decision that is "ours" to make. Suggest a different dress, agenda, restaurant, route. We room alone when we travel. We plan perfect birthday parties for our children. It might look as though we're simply "trying to be a good mom" or a good friend, but what we often do is arrange other people's lives. Controlling women are "the sort of women," as C. S. Lewis said, "who 'live for others.' You can tell the others by their hunted expression."

Controlling women tend to be very well rewarded in this fallen world of ours. We are the ones to receive corporate promotions. We are the ones put in charge of our women's ministries. Can-Do, Bottom-Line, Get-It-Done kinds of women. Women who have never even considered that our Martha Stewart perfectionism might not be a virtue. We have never considered that by living a controlling and domineering life, we are really refusing to trust our God. And it has also never dawned on us that something precious in us is squelched, diminished, and refused. Something that God has given us to bring to the world.

DESOLATE WOMEN

If on the one side of the spectrum we find that Fallen Eve becomes hard, rigid, and controlling, then on the other side we find women who are desolate, needy, far *too* vulnerable. Women like Ruth Jamison in *Fried Green Tomatoes*. She is naive, lost, bereft of any sense of self. She falls under the abuse of a bad man and hasn't the will to get herself out. Take out the abusive situations and you have a woman like Marianne in *Sense and Sensibility*, who is far too willing to give herself over to an untrustworthy man. She is desperate to be loved. And she ends up heartbroken.

Desolate women are ruled by the aching abyss within them. These are the women who buy books like *Men Who Hate Women and the Women Who Love Them* and *Women Who Love Too Much* and *Codependent No More*. They are consumed by a hunger for relationship. A friend of ours, a young man in his twenties, was lamenting how much his mom calls him. "How often does she call?" I asked, thinking he might be exaggerating. "Every day." Whoa. Every day is too often for a mother to call her adult son who has left home.

Sadly, desolate women also tend to hide their true selves. We are certain that if others really knew us, they wouldn't like us—and we can't risk the loss of a relationship. They might be women like Tulah in *My Big Fat Greek Wedding*, who literally hides behind the counter when an attractive man walks in her café. She hides her beauty behind big glasses (in a day of contacts?), baggy outfits, frumpy hair—all chosen because they do *not* draw attention. Because she does not believe she is worth paying attention to. Desolate women might be busy women who hide behind, "There's so much work to do." That's how the women in my (Stasi's) family learned to handle life.

My mother grew up in rural North Dakota. Her parents spent all the long years of their lives in the same house that she was born in. Her father was a cold, detached man. He never spoke the words that little girls long—no, *need*—to hear. She never heard from her father that she was precious or pretty. He never even told her that he loved her. Not once. After one terrible day at school, she ran home with tears streaming down her face. Deeply hurt, sobbing, with her little girl's heart broken, she risked running to her father for comfort. He pushed her away.

Her mother, she knew, loved her. Yet she was not expressive

either. But she was clean . . . and incredibly controlling. My mom was not allowed to have friends over to her house to play because they would mess it up. The living room was not for living in but for looking at. All objects in the house belonged to her mother, and it was not okay to touch them or, heaven forbid, move them. You can imagine, there was no romping in that house. There was no fort building or game playing or dashing about. It was orderly, neat . . . and soul killing.

One day, while her mother was entertaining guests, my own mother was upstairs using the bathroom. A very good girl, she washed her hands in the sink after first closing the drain as she was taught. Then a very bad thing happened. She could not get the water to turn off, or the plug to open. Both were stuck. In a house of rigid rules, one did not interrupt one's parents while they spoke with adults. My mom didn't know what to do. The water ran on. Something was broken. My mom was responsible. She was going to get into trouble. The water was rising. So my mom did what we all do when we are afraid that we have failed and are going to be found out. She hid.

She left the bathroom, went into her bedroom, crawled under her bed, and there she stayed—hiding, cowering, afraid. The water in the sink finally overflowed, spilling onto the floor, soaking through the ceiling, and dripped onto her mother's guests. Oops. Her hiding, like our hiding, only made matters worse.

I was afraid because I was naked; so I hid. (Gen. 3:10)

One of my college roommates was a very pretty young woman, but she didn't know it. She was kind and funny, intelligent and bright. She was also timid and afraid. She spent her evenings camped out in front of her personal television. Declining invitations to go out, she stayed in, night after night, the weeks turning into months. Wounded, heartbroken in ways I could only guess at, she found solace in sitcoms and snacks. Too insecure to enter into the world, she hid from it instead, venturing out only to attend classes and restock her food supply.

Hiding women are those of us who never speak up at a Bible study or PTA council or any kind of meeting. Who, when we pass a beautiful dress in a window, say to ourselves, "I could never wear that." We stay busy at family gatherings and parties we can't avoid. We'd rather go to a movie than out to dinner with a friend. We don't initiate sex with our husbands ever. We dismiss every compliment. We relinquish major decisions to others.

Like Eve after she tasted the forbidden fruit, we women hide. We hide behind our makeup. We hide behind our humor. We hide with angry silences and punishing withdrawals. We hide our truest selves and offer only what we believe is wanted, what is safe. We act in self-protective ways and refuse to offer what we truly see, believe, and know. We will not risk rejection or looking like a fool. We have spoken in the past and been met with blank stares and mocking guffaws. We will not do it again. We hide because we are afraid. We have been wounded and wounded deeply. People have sinned against us and we have sinned as well. To hide means to remain safe, to hurt less. At least that is what we think. And so by hiding, we take matters into our own hands. We don't return to our God with our broken and desperate hearts. And it has never occurred to us that in all our hiding, something precious in us is also squelched, diminished, and refused—something God needs so very, very much for us to bring to the world.

INDULGING

Whether we tend to dominate and control, or withdraw in our desolation and hide, still . . . the ache remains. The deep longings in our hearts as women just won't go away. And so we indulge.

We buy ourselves something nice when we aren't feeling appreciated. We "allow" ourselves a second helping of ice cream or a super-sized something when we are lonely. We move into a fantasy world to find some water for our thirsty hearts. Romance novels (a billion-dollar industry), soap operas, talk shows, gossip, the myriads of women's magazines all feed an inner life of relational dreaming and voyeurism that substitutes—for a while—for the real thing. But none of these really satisfy, and so we find ourselves trying to fill the remaining emptiness with our little indulgences (we call them "bad habits"). Brent Curtis calls them our "little affairs of the heart." God calls them "broken cisterns" (Jer. 2:13). They are what we give our hearts away to instead of giving them to the heart of God.

We daydream our way through traffic. We imagine meaningful conversations or difficult ones where we speak brilliantly. We spend our imaginations on cheap novels, picturing ourselves as the heroine—winsome, pursued, beautiful. We are endlessly creative in our indulgent pursuits, our adulteries of the heart. Certainly, we do not limit ourselves to just one.

Take a moment and consider yours. Where do you go instead of to God when the ache of your heart begins to make itself known? Spending too much money, gambling, bingeing, purging, shopping, drinking, working, cleaning, exercising, too many movies, sitcoms, talk shows, even our negative emotions can become indulgences. When we camp our hearts in self-doubt, condemning thoughts, or even shame because those emotions have become familiar and comfortable, we are faithlessly indulging rather than allowing our deep ache to draw us to God.

Unfortunately, our indulgences make us feel better . . . for a while. They seem to "work," but really only increase our need to indulge again. This is the nightmare of addiction. But it goes far beyond "drugs." We give our hearts to all sorts of other "lovers" that demand our attention, demand we indulge again. When we taste something that we think is good, our longings cease to ache, for a minute, but later we find ourselves empty once more, needing to be filled again and again.

The ways we find to numb our aches, our longings, and our pain are not benign. They are malignant. They entangle themselves in our souls like a cancer and, once attached, become addictions that are both cruel and relentless. Though we seek them out for a little relief from the sorrows of life, addictions turn on us and imprison us in chains that separate us from the heart of God and others as well. It is a lonely prison of our own making, each chain forged in the fire of our indulgent choice. Yet, "Our lovers have so intertwined themselves with our identity that to give them up feels like personal death . . . We wonder if it is possible to live without them" *(The Sacred Romance)*. Yes, we are, each of us, to greater and lesser degrees, still in bondage. But the good news is that "God has not deserted us in our bondage" (Ezra 9:9).

We need not be ashamed that our hearts ache; that we need and thirst and hunger for much more. All of our hearts ache. All of our hearts are at some level unsatisfied and longing. It is our insatiable need for more that drives us to our God. What we need to see is that all our controlling and our hiding, all our indulging, actually serves to separate us from our hearts. We lose touch with those longings that make us women. And the substitutes never, ever resolve the deeper issue of our souls.

EVE'S LINGERING FEAR

Every woman knows now that she is not what she was meant to be. And she fears that soon it will be known—if it hasn't already been discovered—and that she will be abandoned. Left alone to die a death of the heart. That is a woman's worst fear—abandonment. (Isn't it?) Rather than turning back to God, reversing the posture

Captivating

that brought about our crisis in the first place (which Eve set in
motion and we have repeated *ad nauseum*), we continue down that
path by doing what we can to secure ourselves in a dangerous and
unpredictable world.

And down in the depths of our hearts, our Question remains.
Unanswered. Or rather, it remains answered in the way it was
answered so badly in our youth. *Am I lovely? Do you see me? Do you
want to see me? Are you captivated by what you find in me?* We live
haunted by that Question, yet unaware that it still needs an answer.

When we were young, we knew nothing about Eve and what
she did and how it affected us all. We do not first bring our heart's
Question to God, and too often, before we can, we are given
answers in a very painful way. We are wounded into believing horrid things about ourselves. And so every woman comes into the
world set up for a terrible heartbreak.

CHAPTER FOUR

Wounded

✤

These words are razors to my wounded heart.
—WILLIAM SHAKESPEARE

*Ah, Women, that you should be moving
here, among us, grief-filled,
no more protected than we.*
— RAINER MARIA RILKE

*C*arrie woke on her sixth birthday to the sound of singing.

She knew instantly that it was her birthday, *her very own day.* She opened her eyes to discover that balloons had been tied all around her bed—a colorful canopy. The celebration had begun. Her mom was standing by her bedside, holding a coffee cake with a lit candle in it, and her dad was there too, and both of them were singing, "Haaappy Biiirthdaaay tooo youuuu!" Oh, unhindered joy! Squeals of delight, kisses, hugs, and "hoorays!" welcomed her into this day—just as she had been welcomed into the world six years earlier. Her father whispered to his "Little Princess" that he loved her. Her mother reminded her again of how happy she was to have such a wonderful daughter.

There was no doubt about it—this little girl was delighted in.

Life for Carrie was closer to life as God meant it to be for every little girl. She *knew* that her father cherished her. She was his princess. He was her knight in shining armor. He wanted to spend time with her. Carrie *knew* her mother loved her and wanted her. Hers was a world where her father protected her, her mother nurtured her, and she was *enjoyed*. This is the soil a girl's soul was meant to grow in; this was the garden her young heart was meant to flourish within. Every little girl should be so loved, so welcomed—seen, known, treasured. From this place she can become a strong and beautiful and confident woman.

If only that was how it was for all of us.

MOTHERS, FATHERS, AND THEIR DAUGHTERS

For many centuries women lived in close fellowship with other women—gathering at the well, down by the river, preparing meals—many occasions for femininity to just sort of naturally pass from older women to younger women. Our intuition, our keen eye for relationship, our ability to grasp matters of the heart made any sort of formal "passage" into femininity unnecessary. Nowadays those opportunities are nearly gone. When we meet as women, it tends to be in high-stress situations—corporate meetings with deadlines, ministry meetings with agendas, PTA meetings with concerns. The home is the only place left for this vital transmission of feminine identity.

The way you see yourself now, as a grown woman, was shaped early in your life, in the years when you were a little girl. We learned what it meant to be feminine—and *if* we were feminine—while we were very young. Women learn from their mothers what it means to be a woman, and from their fathers the value that a woman has— the value *they* have as a woman. If a woman is comfortable with her own femininity, her beauty, her strength, then the chances are good that her daughter will be too.

From our mothers we receive many, many things, but foremost among them are mercy and tenderness. When my sons were young and got hurt, their dad would say something encouraging like, "Cool wound." I would hold them close and tend their injuries. Our mothers show us the merciful face of God. We are nurtured at their breasts and cradled in their arms. They rock us to sleep and sing us lullabies. Our youngest years are lived within the proximity of their apron strings, and they care for us in all the meanings of the word. When we get hurt, moms kiss us and make it better.

Moms are a bit of a mystery to young girls but also belong to a club that one day they will join. So little girls watch and learn. Little girls learn how to live as women by watching their mothers, their grandmothers, and taking in a myriad of lessons from all the adult women in their lives.

But as for our Question—that is primarily answered by our fathers.

Carrie's father was present to her. He *saw* her, and he made it clear that he enjoyed what he saw. He lavished affection on her with his presence, his protection, his delight. There were names he had for her—secret names only they knew. He called her "Kitten" and "Princess" and "Little Darlin'." Little girls need the tender strength of their fathers. They need to know that their daddies are strong and will protect them; they need to know that their fathers are *for* them. Above all, a little girl learns the answer to her Question from her father.

Remember twirling skirts? We twirled in front of our daddies. We wanted to know, "Daddy, am I lovely? Am I captivating?" From them, we learn that we are delighted in, that we are special . . . or that we are not. How a father relates to his daughter has an enormous effect on her soul—for good or for evil. Numerous studies have shown that women who report a close and caring relationship with their fathers, who received assurance, enjoyment, and approval from them during childhood, suffer less from eating disorders or depression and "developed a strong sense of personal identity and positive self-esteem" (Margo Maine, *Father Hunger*).

But Adam fell, as did Eve, and the fathers and mothers most of us had continued the sad story. They did not provide the things our hearts needed in order to become lovely, vulnerable, strong, adventurous women. No, most of our stories share a different theme.

WOUNDED HEARTS

My friend Sandy was raised in a home with an abusive father and a weak mother. If her dad hit her mother, her mom felt she must have done something to deserve it. When the hitting turned to beating, Sandy came between her father and mother. She tried to stop her dad's cruelty and protect her mom, taking the beating herself. And when her father began to sexually abuse Sandy and her sister, her mother did nothing to protect them; she simply turned away. Sandy's dad began to bring his drunken friends home with him so that they, too, could sexually abuse his daughters. Again and again, her mother did nothing. What do you suppose Sandy learned about masculinity, about femininity, about herself?

Tracey was her parents' second daughter and did not share in the easy intimacy that she saw existed between her father and older sister. She was uncertain about herself, about his feelings for her. On a trip to a water park, she wanted to play with her dad. She asked him to go down the slide with her in the children's area. He didn't want to. Tracey *implored* him to come with her. She was afraid to go alone. She wanted him to catch her at the bottom. She wanted to do it together. He acquiesced. She gleefully walked with him hand in hand to the slide, and he went down first as planned. But it was a children's slide, not made for a grown man, and when he came to the end of it, the water was too shallow for him. The force of his landing broke his foot. He was in pain *and it was her fault.* That's what her young heart believed. What does that teach a girl about her desires and about the effect of her life upon others?

A woman we'll call Melissa told us, "My wound was delivered at birth. My parents had a three-year-old little girl and desperately wanted to have a little boy." You know what's coming. "They brought me to my father for the first time, and he wouldn't even hold me because he was so disappointed I was a girl. I spent my childhood trying to be a good son and prayed each night before I went to bed that I would grow a penis and turn into a boy. Each morning I would wake and check and cry because I was still a girl." How we wish we could say that stories like this are rare. The nature of the assault might be different, but the reason there are so many struggling women is because there were *so* many wounded girls.

Rachel had a verbally abusive father. "I heard everything I suppose a girl can hear. 'You are so stupid. You are worthless. I wish we never had you. You make me sick.' I grew up believing I was repulsive to my father, and I did everything I could to try and make him like me." Abusive fathers are a too common horror. Accomplices, broken mothers, are a painful reality. Both of them often come from abusive homes where the cycle of pain is ruthlessly repeated and passed down.

You cannot be alive very long without being wounded. The sun rises, the stars follow their courses, the waves roll in crashing against the rocks, and we are wounded. Broken hearts cannot long be avoided in this beautiful yet dangerous world we live in. This is not Eden. Not even close. We are not living in the world our souls were made for. Something's rotten in the state of Denmark and in our own backyards as we journey through the unknown terrain of the moments and months that make up our lives.

Take a deep look into the eyes of anyone and behind the smile or the fear, you will find pain. And most people are in more pain than even they realize. Longfellow said, "If we could read the secret histories of our enemies we should find in each man's life sorrow and suffering enough to disarm all hostility." Sorrow is not a stranger to any of us, though only a few have learned that it is not our enemy either. Because we are the ones loved by God, the King of kings, Jesus himself, who came to heal the brokenhearted and set the captives free (Isaiah 61), we can take a look back. We can take his hand and remember. We *must* remember if we would not be held prisoner to the wounds and the messages we received growing up.

The horror that abusive fathers inflict on their daughters wounds their souls to their very core. It breaks their hearts, ushers in shame and ambivalence and a host of defensive strategies that shut down their feminine hearts. But at least the assault is obvious. The pain that absent fathers inflict on their daughters is damaging as well, but far harder to see.

Passive Fathers

As I said earlier, fallen men tend to sin in one of two ways. Either they become driven, violent men—their strength gone bad—or they become passive, silent men (like Adam)—their strength gone away. Lori's dad was present physically but absent in every other way. A little girl longs to be delighted in by her father, but Lori's dad wanted nothing to do with her. When her elementary school held a father/daughter dinner, Lori *desperately* wanted to go. She invited her father to go; she begged him to come, but he would have none of it. Lori assumed he did not want to attend because he was ashamed to be seen with her.

As many little girls do, Lori took ballet lessons. She felt so pretty in her pink leotard and tights that she asked her father to please come and watch her dance. He answered her that when she was on a real stage, then he would come and watch her. As you

might know, dance classes end with recitals, and so, the day did come for little Lori to dance on a real stage. Pretty in her shimmering costume, she eagerly waited and watched for her father's arrival. He never came. Later that evening friends of her father had to carry him into the house, as he was too drunk to walk in by himself. Lori's little-girl heart believed her dad had gone to great lengths in order *not* to have to watch her dance.

Debbie's father had an affair when she was young. He was not a violent man. There was nothing abusive about him. In fact, he was kind to her mother, as he was to Debbie and her sister. They shared Sunday dinners, went to church together. Only, he chose another woman. "I guess she wasn't enough to keep him," Debbie said about her mother. Then she paused and said, "I guess *we* weren't enough to keep him." Affairs and divorces strike at a woman's worst fear—abandonment. They wound, not just the mothers, but the daughters as well. The wound is sometimes hard to identify because the transgression seemed to be against his wife. But what does the girl learn?

Laurie's father divorced her mom when she was six. In her heart, *she* was being divorced too. "They tried to talk about it with us, make it all sound mature and like it's going to be okay. But he was leaving." Her father did come for visits, to take her on outings. But she learned to hide her heart from him. "I learned to cry underwater. When we'd go to the pool, I didn't want him to see me crying." So many girls learned something like this. Hide your vulnerability. Hide your heart. You aren't safe.

My (Stasi's) father was absent much of my youth. He was a man raised to be strong and good. In his era, the primary way a man showed his strength was in providing for his family. But like too many men, my dad worked long hours to provide for us financially and yet withheld the thing we needed most: himself. My father was a traveling salesman. He would be gone for three weeks at a time

and then be home for a weekend before leaving again. An alcoholic, he often stopped off at the local bar or a neighbor's house to hoist a few before coming in our door. When he was present physically, he was absent emotionally, preferring the company of the television and a glass of scotch to his family. He did not know me. I guess he didn't want to.

MOTHER WOUNDS

My mom was a lonely and busy woman. When I was young I had to pretend to be sick in order to get a morsel of her attention. I remember sitting at the kitchen table as a young girl watching her make dinner when she told me for the first time—but not the last—how devastated she was when she learned that she was pregnant with me. I was the last of four children, too close together, and she wept when she found out that I, the daughter of an overwhelmed mother and an absent father, was coming. You can imagine the effect that has on a little girl's heart.

Chris's dad was not absent. He was, in fact, deeply involved in her life. She loved horses, had a natural gift with them, and he was very proud of her gift. He delighted in her riding abilities and encouraged her to pursue them. He was present and supportive, he enjoyed her immensely, and she knew it. And her mother was jealous. She told Chris that her father was just "using" her. She spewed venom that her father was cruel, selfish, and the attention he paid her was wrong. Chris's mom belittled her love for horses, never came to a class or a show, and told Chris that in her riding clothes she looked manly and unattractive.

Dana's mother locked her and her brother and sisters in the closet for hours on end, day after day growing up. Her mother did not trust them nor trust baby sitters, so would put them in the closet while she went out. They were not a poor family, but her

mother bought the cheapest food possible—stale, moldy bread, overripe fruit. Her mother would feed her little, then wake her up at midnight and demand that she eat a piece of bruised, ugly fruit. She was twenty-one years old when she tasted her first perfectly ripe pear and wondered over the flavor.

The stories of these women and the wounds they received as little girls are all different, but the effects of their wounds and the effects of ours are painfully similar. Some of these stories are extreme. The feelings of uncertainty and worthlessness that they breed are not. What was your childhood like? What lessons did you learn as a little girl? What did your parents want from you? Were you delighted in? Did you know to the core of your being that you were loved, special, worth protecting, and wanted? I pray so. But I know that for many of you, the childhood you were meant to have, the childhood you wanted to have, is a far cry from the childhood you *did* have.

THE MESSAGES OF OUR WOUNDS— AND HOW THEY SHAPED US

The wounds that we received as young girls did not come alone. They brought messages with them, messages that struck at the core of our hearts, right in the place of our Question. Our wounds strike at the core of our *femininity*. The damage done to our feminine hearts through the wounds we received is made much worse by the horrible things we believe about ourselves as a result. As children, we didn't have the faculties to process and sort through what was happening to us. Our parents were godlike. We believed them to be right. If we were overwhelmed or belittled or hurt or abused, we believed that somehow it was because of *us*—the problem was with *us*.

Lori's father didn't come to her recital. He went out of his way not to come. That was the wound. The *message* was that she wasn't worth his time. She wasn't worth loving. She felt that there must be something terribly wrong with her. Tracey's father broke his foot. She invited him into her heart's desire, and the result was disaster. The message? "Your desire for relationship causes pain. You are just 'too much.'" And she has spent the last twenty years trying not to be too much, trying to minimize her desires, trying to find some way to be loved without being too much. She has lopped off huge parts of her wonderful personality as a result.

Debbie's father had an affair. What made it confusing was that in many ways, he was a good man. The message that settled in her heart as a teenage girl was, "You'd better do more than she did or you won't keep your man." After this came a young man who pursued Debbie, and then left for no apparent reason. We've known this beautiful young woman for several years now, and one thing has puzzled us—why is she always working on her life? Why is she always trying to "improve" herself? Debbie is always looking for something to work on. Prayer, exercise, financial responsibility, a new hair color, more discipline. Why is she trying so hard? Doesn't she know how amazing she is? What makes her search so frustrating is that she doesn't know what *is* wrong with her. She simply fears that somehow she is not enough.

Many women feel that, by the way. We can't put words to it, but down deep we fear there is something terribly wrong with us. If we were the princess, then our prince would have come. If we were the daughter of a king, he would have fought for us. We can't help but believe that if we were different, if we were *better*, then we would have been loved as we so longed to be. It must be us.

Sandy's father abused her, and her mother turned away. It wrought great evil upon her soul. In all that she learned, Sandy came away with two basic things about femininity: To be a woman is to be powerless; there's nothing good about vulnerability; it's just "weakness." And to be feminine is to draw unwanted intimacy to yourself.

Does it surprise you that she doesn't want to be feminine? Like so many sexually abused women, Sandy finds herself in the awful bind of longing for intimacy (she was created for that) but fearing to look the least bit alluring to a man. She's settled for the persona of the "competent and efficient professional woman," kind but guarded, never too attractive and never, ever, in need and never "weak."

Some women who were sexually abused choose another path. Or, perhaps more honestly, they find themselves compulsively heading in another direction. They never received love, but they did experience some sort of intimacy through the sexual abuse, and now they give themselves over to one man after another, hoping to somehow heal the wrongful sexual encounters with sex that has love to it.

Melissa's mother was a wicked woman who beat her children with a wooden rod. "I was absolutely terrified of my mother," she confessed. "She seemed psychotic and would play evil mind games. Most of the time we never really knew why we were getting beat. My father did nothing. One thing I did know was that with every blow my hatred for her deepened. She turned my sister into a fragile mush of a person, and I vowed she would never do that to me. I vowed that I would be tough, hard, like a rock." This she became, well into her adult life.

The vows we make as children are very understandable—and very, very damaging. They shut our hearts down. They are essentially a deep-seated agreement with the messages of our wounds. They act as an agreement with the verdict on us. "Fine. If that's how it is, then that's how it is. I'll live my life in the following way . . ."

It's taken a lot of years for me to sort through the wounds and messages that shaped my life. It's been a journey for growing clarity, understanding, and healing. Just last night, as John and I talked about this chapter, I began to realize more clearly what the message of my wounds has been. My mom was overwhelmed with the prospect of having another child—me. The message that landed in my heart was that I was overwhelming; my presence alone caused sorrow and pain. From a father who didn't seem to want to know me or be with me, I got the message, "You don't have a beauty that captivates me. You are a disappointment."

When I was a little girl, I would hide in the closet. No one was looking for me; it was just that I felt safer in there. I began this hiding when I was ten years old—the same year that my family fell apart. We had been living in Kansas in a neighborhood that was everything you would want a neighborhood to be. My sisters, brother, and I played with the neighborhood kids. No one had fences back then, and all was open range. And school was a place we flourished. I was voted "Citizen of the Year." My oldest sister was chosen as a foreign exchange student and was supposed to go to France. My next sister was the star of the school play. My brother was popular and won awards for achievement. You get the picture. It was good.

And then, we moved (the result of a promotion for my father), and it was like an atom bomb went off in our family. We had a huge support system in Kansas, much larger and stronger than we had realized. Friends, neighbors, teachers, all were holding us up. When we moved, we no longer had that support, and my family was not strong enough on its own; we fell down like a house of cards. Though my father no longer traveled as much, he worked long hours, often leaving the house before we arose and coming home long after we had fallen asleep. I would think he was away on a business trip far from home when in reality he was just an hour's drive away. Dad was an alcoholic and was also diagnosed as bipolar, so when he was home, you never knew which father you were going to get. Would it be the happy dad or the raging father?

Our home was no longer a refuge but became a battleground. Meals together often ended with angry words and hot tears. My father's drinking increased, matched only by my mother's escalating pain and resentment. When they were together, barbs flew through the air like poison darts. In an effort to escape, my brother stole a car and tried to drive back to Kansas where life was good. My mother left to stay with her parents for a while, and one of my sisters ran away. Going out to dinner with my father one night, he had too much to drink and began flirting with the waitress, asking for her phone number. It was all too much for my young, lonely heart. Back home, I went to the medicine cabinet and swallowed all the pills I thought necessary to end my life and my pain. I woke the next morning, grateful that I hadn't died, but keenly aware that my world was no longer safe.

And so, I made a vow. Somewhere in my young heart, without even knowing I was doing it or putting words to it, I vowed to protect myself by never causing pain, never requiring attention. My job in the family was to be invisible, to cause no waves. If I upset things at all, surely this ship would sink. So I began to hide. I hid my needs, my desires, my very heart. I hid my true self. And when it was all too much, I hid in the closet.

Fast-forward fourteen years. I am now a newlywed, married to a strong and forthright husband who is not afraid of confrontation, welcomes it even. We would be sitting at the kitchen table and if the conversation became tense, I was out of there. He would come looking for me. "Stasi, where are you?" Where was I? I was hiding in the closet. Literally.

I was embarrassed by my young behavior, felt foolish about my seeming inability to talk maturely through a disagreement. But I had never seen it done, and I didn't know how. John's slightest disappointment in something I had done triggered my unhealed heart. It took many, many months for John's love and reassurance to begin to penetrate my frightened heart. I still remember the first time we were in the middle of a disagreement, and I was able to stay with him in the room. It took all of my will to keep one foot in the room while the other straddled the doorway of the bathroom, ready to retreat into contrived safety. It was a turning point. I've never hidden *in that way* again.

I did, however, begin to put on weight faster than you would think humanly possible. Unconsciously, I had found a new way to hide. I feared from the start of my marriage that at my core I was—and would always be—a disappointment to John; that it was simply a matter of time before he realized it. (The message of my wound.) The wounded little girl inside thought it would be better to hide. And my hiding, like your hiding, made things much, much worse. John and I have had many years of pain. As Jesus said, she who seeks to save her life will lose it (Matt. 16:25). *The vows we make and the things we do as a result of our wounds only make matters worse.*

WOUNDED FEMININITY

As a result of the wounds we receive growing up, we come to believe that some part of us, maybe every part of us, is marred. Shame enters in and makes its crippling home deep within our hearts. Shame is what makes us look away, so we avoid eye contact with strangers and friends. Shame is that feeling that haunts us, the sense that if someone really knew us, they would shake their heads in disgust and run away. Shame makes us feel, no, *believe*, that we do not measure up—not to the world's standards, the church's standards, or our own standards.

Others seem to master their lives, but shame grips our hearts and pins them down, ever ready to point out our failures and judge our worth. We are lacking. We know we are not all that we long to be, all that God longs for us to be, but instead of coming up for grace-filled air and asking God what he thinks of us, shame keeps us pinned down and gasping, believing that we deserve to suffocate.

If we were not deemed worthy of love as children, it is incredibly difficult to believe we are worth loving as adults. Shame says we are unworthy, broken, and beyond repair.

Shame causes us to hide. We are afraid of being truly seen, and so we hide our truest selves and offer only what we believe is wanted. If we are a dominating kind of woman, we offer our "expertise." If we are a desolate kind of woman, we offer our "service." We are silent and do not say what we see or know when it is different from what others are saying, because we think we must be wrong. We refuse to bring the weight of our lives, who God has made us to be, to bear on others out of a fear of being rejected.

Shame makes us feel very uncomfortable with our beauty. Women are beautiful, every single one of us. It is one of the glorious ways that we bear the image of God. But few of us believe we are beautiful, and fewer still are comfortable with it. We either think we don't have any beauty or if we do, that it's dangerous and bad. So we hide our beauty behind extra weight and layers of unnecessary makeup. Or we neutralize our beauty by putting up protective, defensive walls that warn others to keep their distance.

An Unholy Alliance

Over the years we've come to see that the only thing *more* tragic than the things that have happened to us is what we have done with them.

Words were said, painful words. Things were done, awful things. And they shaped us. Something inside of us *shifted*. We embraced the messages of our wounds. We accepted a twisted view of ourselves. And from that we chose a way of relating to our world. We made a vow never to be in that place again. We adopted strategies to protect ourselves from being hurt again. A woman who is living out of a broken, wounded heart is a woman who is living a self-protective life. She may not be aware of it, but it is true. It's our way of trying to "save ourselves."

We also developed ways of trying to get something of the love our hearts cried out for. The ache is there. Despite the best face we put on our lives, the ache is there. As Proverbs says, "Even in laughter the heart may ache" (14:13). Our desperate need for love and affirmation, our thirst for some taste of romance and adventure and beauty is there. So we turned to boys or to food or to romance novels; we lost ourselves in our work or at church or in some sort of service. All this adds up to the women we are today. Much of what we call our "personalities" is actually the mosaic of our choices for self-protection plus our plan to get something of the love we were created for.

The problem is our plan has nothing to do with God.

The wounds we received and the messages they brought formed a sort of unholy alliance with our fallen nature as women. From Eve we received a deep mistrust in the heart of God toward us. Clearly, he's holding out on us. We'll just have to arrange for the life we want. We will control our world. But there is also an ache deep within, an ache for intimacy and for life. We'll have to find a way to fill it. A way that does not require us to trust anyone, especially God. A way that will not require vulnerability.

In some ways, this is every little girl's story, here in this world east of Eden.

But the wounds don't stop once we are grown up. Some of the most crippling and destructive wounds we receive come much later in our lives. The wounds that we have received over our lifetimes have not come to us in a vacuum. There is, in fact, a *theme* to them, a pattern. The wounds you have received have come to you for a purpose from one who knows all you are meant to be and fears you.

CHAPTER FIVE

A Special Hatred

❦

All who hate me whisper about me,
imagining the worst for me.
—PSALM 41:7 NLT

Take away this murdherin' hate, an' give us
Thine own eternal love.
—SEAN O'CASEY

The storm is over now. And Stasi is weeping. She had poured so much love and care into her garden over the years. Many, many hours lovingly given to creating a place of remarkable beauty. Special choices were made; seedlings transplanted with care, fertilizing, mulching, weeding. She pruned and watered and sprayed for aphids. She moved plants, replaced them, looking for the right feel to it all. The result was stunning. People would walk up our path, stop, and just behold—it was so lovely. Wild roses, lavender and delphiniums, fountain grasses, Shasta daisies—more color and texture than I could describe. A place of rest and solace, a refuge from the world. A whiff of Eden.

Until tonight.

The hail began about 6 p.m. At first, it didn't seem that threatening. Summer brings a few hail showers each year in the Rockies, pea-sized balls lasting only about ten minutes. The hail this time began the size of marbles; after fifteen minutes it began to come in the size of golf balls, pouring down like Noah's flood turned to ice. For forty minutes it came, relentlessly, stripping branches off trees, laying waste to all living things like some Old Testament plague. And when it finally passed on over the mountain, Stasi's garden was destroyed.

I stood looking out the window in shock and grief. Summer is so short here; there are just a few months even to enjoy flowers and greenery. But this—this was an *assault*. Beauty ravaged beyond recognition. As we talked about the devastation, both of us turned in our thoughts . . . to Eve. This ruin of a garden is a picture, a terribly fitting metaphor of what has happened to the Crown of Creation. How much more the grief and how much greater the loss when it is the life and heart of a woman.

Yes, women have fallen from grace. Yes, they have been wounded. But in order to understand the lingering doubts in your own heart regarding your femininity, in order to understand why it is so rare to encounter a truly alive and vibrant woman, you must hear more of the story.

FURTHER ASSAULT

By the time I was a teenager—a girl becoming a young woman—I had pretty much divorced myself from my family. My oldest sister had moved to Europe. (She went for a three-month "vacation." She stayed seven years. That tells you something about what life was like in our home.) My brother had moved out, as had my other sister. I was left at home to finish high school. My parents began to give me some of the attention I craved as a girl, but it was too little, too late. My heart had already checked out. It was well hidden. Before them I lived the life of a "smart and good student." Out of sight I lived quite another life.

I used alcohol and drugs to numb the pain of my wounds. And, as so many other young women do whose hearts have been badly missed or intentionally wounded by their fathers, I turned to boys, then to men for love. At least, I convinced myself, I was wanted for *something*, if only for a night.

I went to Europe my last summer of college. I was enamored by the ancient beauty I experienced as well as by my boundless freedom. But a young, rebellious, unwise woman set loose with a Eurail Pass and a bleeding heart attracted cruel attention. While traveling through Italy, I was sexually assaulted, and although I was furious at the man, deep in my heart I felt somehow worthy of assault. I believed that I had brought it on myself. I agreed with the enemy of my soul that I was a horrid person, and that I deserved only pain. Later, in the south of France, I unwittingly put myself in a dangerous position. After enjoying a few too many drinks at a local bar, my girlfriend and I accepted a ride back to the hotel from the men we had been drinking with. You must be shaking your head as you read this, knowing what was coming. I am. Their offered ride did not lead us back to the hotel but instead to a private location where I was raped.

After the assault, I went into a state of shock. I remember discovering new bruises and scrapes with a sense of unbelief. But I was not enraged; I was terrified. I felt indignation toward my violators—but deeper, a sense of shame and self-loathing. I wanted to be a good woman. I wanted to be a valiant woman. I wanted to be a strong woman. But I felt nothing of the kind. I bought and wore a necklace I loved. It was the symbol for woman with a fist in the middle. I wore the necklace as a proud feminist to show my independence and strength—and I hid in my hotel room. I was terrified of men and terrified of my beauty. Beauty was dangerous. I believed it had attracted the assaults; it had caused me unspeakable pain and with it, as too many women know, unrelenting shame.

When I returned to school, I told my boyfriend what had happened to me. His response was, "You probably brought it on yourself." We had, as you can tell, an unhealthy relationship. He was verbally abusive and angry. I received no compassion from him, no words of comfort. He wasn't even angry at my assailants. The messages from my childhood wounds were painfully reinforced. "Hide your heart. You are a disappointment. You are worthless. No one cares. No one wants to care. You are alone."

If you will listen carefully to any woman's story, you will hear a theme: the assault on her heart. It might be obvious as in the stories of physical, verbal, or sexual abuse. Or it might be more subtle, the indifference of a world that cares nothing for her but *uses* her until she is drained. Forty years of being neglected damages a woman's heart too, dear friends. Either way, the wounds continue to come long after we've "grown up," but they all seem to speak the same message. Our Question is answered again and again throughout our lives, the message driven home into our hearts like a stake.

Melissa was the young girl we told you about whose mother beat her with a two-by-four. She eventually got out of the house, at the age of nineteen.

I married a man who was going to be a youth pastor. I thought I had to marry this man since I was so repulsive and would never get another chance. No one else would want me. I was a virgin when I married and [loved] giving myself to my husband as the ultimate gift. The morning after we were married, I snuggled close to my husband and began to kiss him. He pushed me away and told me he wasn't in the mood. After our wedding night we didn't have sex again for over a week. He didn't touch me or even seem the least bit interested in me. I was devastated! And again my question was answered the exact same way.

As women we tend to feel that "it must be me." That's the effect of our early wounds. "Something is fundamentally wrong with me." So many women feel that way. (Why are we working so hard to improve ourselves? Or why do we keep so busy that the issues of our hearts never have to come to the surface?) We also feel that we are essentially alone. And that somehow the two are related. We believe we are alone because we are not the women we should be.

We don't feel worthy of pursuit. So we hang a Do Not Disturb sign on our personalities, send a "back off" message to the world. Or we desperately seek pursuit, losing all self-respect in an emotional and physical promiscuity. We don't feel that we are irreplaceable, so we try and make ourselves useful. We don't believe we are beautiful, so we work hard to be outwardly beautiful *or* we "let ourselves go" and hide behind a persona that has no allure. We try so hard, and in so many ways, to protect our hearts from further pain.

What Is Really Going On Here?

I was sleeping when the attack on Disa started. I was taken away by the attackers, they were all in uniforms. They took dozens of other girls and made us walk for three hours. During the day we were beaten and they were telling us: "You, the black women, we will exterminate you, you have no god." At night we were raped several times. The Arabs guarded us with arms and we were not given food for three days. (Sudanese Woman, quoted in *Amnesty International report*)

The story of the treatment of women down through the ages is not a noble history. It has noble moments in it, to be sure, but taken as a whole, women have endured what seems to be a special hatred ever since we left Eden. The story we just cited is but one of thousands coming not just out of the Sudan but from many war-torn countries like it. UN Peacekeeping troops say that in 2009 alone, in the war raging in the Congo, more than 7,500 rapes were reported. They know the actual number is much higher. Sexual assault is a far too common and effective weapon in these "civil" wars. Honestly, what do you make of the degradation, the abuse, and the open assault that women around the world have endured—are enduring even now?

Up until about seventy years ago, little girls born in China who were not left by the side of the road to die (boys are the preferred child) often had their feet bound to keep them small. Small feet were a sign of feminine beauty and were prized by would-be husbands. They were also crippling, which is quite possibly another reason why men thought them a good thing. Women who had their feet bound as children hobbled in pain throughout their lives, unable to walk freely or quickly. Although the practice was outlawed in the 1930s, it continued long after.

You might know that through the thousands of years of Jewish history recorded in the Old Testament, Jewish women were considered property with no legal rights (as they were and are in many cultures). They were not allowed to study the Law, nor to formally educate their children. They had a segregated place in the synagogue. It was common practice for a Jewish man to add to his morning prayers, "Thank you, God, for not making me a Gentile, a woman, or a slave."

A Chinese proverb says that "a woman should be like water; she should take no form and have no voice." An Indian proverb says, "Educating a woman is like watering your neighbor's garden," meaning, of course, that educating a woman is both foolish and a waste of time. In Hinduism, a woman has less value than a cow. We are not talking ancient history here. We are talking about today. Now. In Islam, a woman requires three men to verify her story in court in order for her testimony to be valid. Her testimony, her worth, is one third of a man's.

The story goes well beyond the denial of education and legal rights. Clitoridectomy is the removal, or circumcision, of the clitoris. A painful, horrible practice, female genital mutilation continues today and is performed on girls when they reach about five years old. Done primarily in Africa, the surgery is often performed in the wilderness with the use of a sharp rock. Infections are common. Sometimes the girl dies. A woman is forever maimed, never able to enjoy sexual pleasure—and that is the point. A sexually aware woman is thought to be dangerous. Femininity must be controlled.

Sexual violence against women is rampant throughout the world. It is also rampant against little girls. More than one million *girls* are sold into the sex trade every year. Dear God—what is to account for the systemic, often brutal, nearly universal assault on women? Where does this *come* from? Do not make the mistake of believing that "men are the enemy." Certainly men have had a hand in this, and will have a day of reckoning before their Maker. But you will not understand this story—or *your* story—until you begin to see the actual Forces behind this and get a grip on their motives.

Where does this hatred for women, seen all over the world, come from? Why is it so *diabolical*?

A SPECIAL HATRED

For we are not fighting against people made of flesh and blood, but against the evil rulers and authorities of the unseen world, against those mighty powers of darkness who rule this world, and against wicked spirits in the heavenly realms. (Eph. 6:12 NLT)

The assault on femininity—its long history, its utter viciousness—cannot be understood apart from the spiritual forces of evil we are warned against in the Scriptures. This is not to say that men (and women, for they, too, assault women) have no accountability in their treatment of women. Not at all. It is simply to say that no explanation for the assault upon Eve and her daughters is sufficient unless it opens our eyes to the Prince of Darkness and his special hatred of femininity.

Turn your attention again to the events that took place in the garden of Eden. Notice—who does the Evil One go after? Who does Satan single out for his move against the human race? He could have chosen Adam . . . but he didn't. Satan went after Eve. He set his sights on *her*. Have you ever wondered why? It might have been that he, like any predator, chose what he believed to be the weaker of the two. There is some truth to that. He is utterly ruthless. But we believe there is more. Why does Satan make Eve the focus of his assault on humanity?

You may know that Satan was first named Lucifer, or Son of the Morning. It infers a glory, a brightness or radiance unique to him. In the days of his former glory he was appointed a guardian angel. Many believe he was the captain of the angel armies of God. The guardian of the glory of the Lord.

> You were the model of perfection,
> full of wisdom and perfect in beauty.
> You were in Eden,
> the garden of God;
> every precious stone adorned you:
> ruby, topaz and emerald,
> chrysolite, onyx and jasper,
> sapphire, turquoise and beryl.
> Your settings and mountings were made of gold;
> on the day you were created they were prepared.
> You were anointed as a guardian cherub,

for so I ordained you.
You were on the holy mount of God;
you walked among the fiery stones. (Ezek. 28:12–14)

Perfect in beauty. That is the key. Lucifer was gorgeous. He was breathtaking. And it was his ruin. Pride entered Lucifer's heart. The angel came to believe he was being cheated somehow. He craved the worship that was being given to God for himself. He didn't merely want to play a noble role in the Story; he wanted the Story to be about *him*. He wanted to be the star. He wanted the attention, the adoration for himself. ("Mirror, Mirror, on the wall . . .")

Your heart became proud
on account of your beauty,
and you corrupted your wisdom
because of your splendor. (Ezek. 28:17)

Satan fell *because* of his beauty. Now his heart for revenge is to assault beauty. He destroys it in the natural world wherever he can. Strip mines, oil spills, fires, Chernobyl. He wreaks destruction on the glory of God in the earth like a psychopath committed to destroying great works of art.

But *most* especially, he hates Eve.

Because she is captivating, uniquely glorious, and he cannot be. She is the incarnation of the Beauty of God. More than anything else in all creation, she embodies the glory of God. She allures the world to God. He hates it with a jealousy we can only imagine.

And there is more. The Evil One also hates Eve because she gives life. Women give birth, not men. Women nourish life. And they also bring life into the world soulfully, relationally, spiritually—in everything they touch. Satan was a murderer from the beginning (John 8:44). He brings death. His is a kingdom of death. Ritual sacrifices, genocide, the Holocaust, abortion—those are his ideas. And thus Eve is his greatest human threat, for she brings life. She is a lifesaver and a life giver. Eve means "life" or "life producer." "Adam named his wife Eve, because she would become the mother of all the living" (Gen. 3:20).

Put those two things together—that Eve incarnates the Beauty of God *and* she gives life to the world. Satan's bitter heart cannot bear it. He assaults her with a special hatred. History removes any doubt about this. Do you begin to see it?

Think of the great stories—in nearly all of them, the villain goes after the Hero's true love. He turns his sights on the *Beauty*. Magua goes after Cora in *The Last of the Mohicans*. Longshanks goes after Murron in *Braveheart*. Commodus goes after Maximus's wife in *Gladiator*. The Witch attacks Sleeping Beauty. The stepsisters assault Cinderella. Satan goes after Eve.

This explains an awful lot. It is not meant to scare you. Actually, it will shed so much light on your life's story, if you will let it. Most of you thought the things that have happened to you were somehow *your fault*—that you deserved it. If only you had been prettier or smarter or done more or pleased them, somehow it wouldn't have happened. You would have been loved. They wouldn't have hurt you.

And most of you are living with the guilt that somehow it's your fault you aren't more deeply pursued now. That you do not have an essential role in a great adventure. That you have no beauty to unveil. The message of our wounds nearly always is, "This is because of you. This is what you deserve." It changes things to realize that, no, it is because you are *glorious* that these things happened. It is because you are powerful. It is because you are a major threat to the kingdom of darkness. Because you uniquely carry the glory of God to the world.

You are hated *because* of your beauty and power.

On a Human Level

I (John) have a confession to make: I didn't want to coauthor this book.

Oh, I thought it *ought* to be written. It needed to be written. I just didn't want to be the one to do it. I knew it would require me to enter into the world of women—and into *my* woman's world—in a far deeper way than daily life requires of me. To do any sort of justice to a book for women would require me to go deeper, listen even more carefully, study, delve into the mystery (okay—bloody mess) of a woman's soul. Part of me just didn't want to go there. I had what felt like an allergic reaction. Pull back. Withdraw.

I was keenly aware of this going on inside me, and I felt like a jerk. But I also knew enough about myself and about the battle for a woman's heart that I needed to explore this ambivalence. What is this thing in me—and in most men—that just doesn't want to go deep into a woman's world? "You are too much. Too hard. It's too much work. Men are simpler. Easier." And isn't that just the message you've lived with all your life as a woman? "You're too much, and not enough. You're just not worth the effort." ("And why is it such an effort? There must be something wrong with you.")

Now, part of a man's fundamental reluctance to truly dive into the world of a woman comes from a man's deepest fear, failure. Oh, he may joke about "the differences of men and women," Mars and Venus and all that. But the truth is, he is afraid. He fears that having delved into his woman's world, he won't have what it takes to help her there. That is his sin. That is his cowardice. And because of her shame, most of the time a man gets away with it. Most marriages (and long-term dating relationships) reach this sort of unspoken settlement. "I'm not coming any closer. This is as far as I'm willing to go. But I won't leave, and that ought to make you happy." And so there is this sort of détente, a cordial agreement to live only so close.

The effect is that most women feel alone.

Some of this is simply selfishness on the part of men. Lord knows men are selfish and self-centered. When Eve was first assaulted, Adam didn't do jack squat. Men sin through violence and through *passivity*. It's that plain and simple . . . and ugly.

But there is something else. There is something even more diabolical at work here. We had an amazing meeting a few months ago that proved to be—for me at least—a surprise unveiling of this mystery.

Stasi and I had gathered with the men and women in our ministry who do the men's and women's retreats. The men's team wanted to offer our counsel and support and prayer to the women's team for their upcoming event. It was a chance for the women—and all of them are really, really amazing women—to just sort of open their hearts to us and process how things were going.

Our gathering moved rather quickly from external kinds of issues—how long the sessions should be and logistical stuff like that—to the internal world of the women's team themselves. As we began to talk more intimately, something started coming over me. Just a sense, an inexplicable but strong impression.

Back off.

That's what I felt. No one said it; nothing they were doing implied it; it wasn't a voice in my head. Just a very strong impression. I wasn't sure where it was coming from, but this strong "reluctance," this sense of *maybe we shouldn't press further into this*, this feeling of just *back off* was growing in me, or over me, every moment we moved more deeply into their lives. With every step we took *toward* their hearts, I felt a stronger impression to end the conversation, withdraw, bail out. Watching this unfold, I knew I was onto something big.

I knew that, as a man, this *wasn't* my heart's true desire toward these women. I love them. I want to fight for them. I have many times. I knew as well it could not be *their* heart's desire. They invited our engagement. So I interrupted the flow of conversation with what seemed like an unrelated question to the women: "Do you feel alone in this?" Silence. Then tears, deep tears, from some deep place within each of them. "Yes," they all said. "We do." But I knew it was more than about the retreats. "Do you feel like that in your lives too, I mean, just generally, as a woman?" "Yes, absolutely. I feel alone most of the time."

Now, you must understand that each of these women have deep and meaningful relationships in their lives. I knew that if *they* felt alone, my God—what must every other woman feel as well? And this strong message of "back off"—if we felt that after years of fighting for them, what must all the other guys out there feel? I bet they haven't ever identified it or put words to it, but I'll guarantee they've felt it . . . and probably just thought it was what they, or their woman, or both of them wanted.

"Back off," or, "Leave her alone," or, "You don't really want to go there—she'll be too much for you" is something Satan has set against every woman from the day of her birth. It's the emotional and spiritual equivalent of leaving a little girl by the side of the road to die. And to every woman he has whispered, "You are alone," or "When they see who you really are, you will be alone," or "No one will ever truly come for you."

Take a moment. Quiet your heart and ask yourself, "Is this a message I have believed, feared, lived with?" Not only do most women fear they will ultimately be abandoned by the men in their lives—they fear it from other women as well. That they will be abandoned by their friends and left alone. It's time to reveal this pervasive threat, this crippling fear, this terrible lie.

I'm reminded of a scene from *The Two Towers*, the second film in

The Lord of the Rings trilogy. It takes place in the land of Rohan, in the hall of the king, in the chambers of the lovely Éowyn. She is the king's niece, the only Lady of the court. Her dearest cousin, Théodred, the son of the king, has just died from wounds he received in battle. She is grieving her loss when Wormtongue—supposed counselor to the king but a treacherous, vile creature—slinks into her chambers and begins to weave his spell around the unprotected maiden.

WORMTONGUE: O . . . he must have died sometime during the night. What a tragedy for the king to lose his only son and heir. I understand his passing is hard to accept. Especially now that your brother has deserted you. [Wormtongue arranged for his banishment.]

ÉOWYN: Leave me alone, snake!

WORMTONGUE: O, but you are alone. Who knows what you have spoken to the darkness in bitter watches of the night when all your life seems to shrink, the walls of your bower closing in about you. A hushed, tremulsome, wild thing. (*He takes her face in his hand.*) So fair . . . and so cold. Like a morning with pale spring, still clinging to winter's chill.

ÉOWYN: (*Finally pulling away from his clutch.*) Your words are poison.

"Oh, but you are alone." This is the way of the Evil One toward you. He plays upon a woman's worst fear: abandonment. He arranges for her to be abandoned, and he puts his spin on every event he can to make it seem like abandonment.

THERE IS HOPE

I am not letting men off the hook. God knows we have a lot more repenting to do. I *am* saying that you won't begin to understand the long and sustained assault on femininity, on women, until you see it as part of something much larger. The most wicked force the world has ever known. The Enemy bears a special hatred for Eve. If you believe he has any role in the history of this world, you cannot help but see it.

The Evil One had a hand in all that has happened to you. If he didn't arrange for the assault directly—and certainly human sin has a large enough role to play—then he made sure he drove the message of the wounds home into your heart. He is the one who has dogged your heels with shame and self-doubt and accusation. He is the one who offers the false comforters to you in order to deepen your bondage. He is the one who has done these things in order to prevent your restoration. For that is what he fears. He fears who you are; what you are; what you might become. He fears your beauty and your life-giving heart.

Now listen to the voice of your King. This is God's heart toward you:

> For Zion's sake I will not keep silent,
> for Jerusalem's sake I will not remain quiet,
>   till her righteousness shines out like the dawn [*until you shimmer*],
>   her salvation like a blazing torch.
> The nations will see your righteousness,
> and all kings your glory [*your beauty*];
> you will be called by a new name
> that the mouth of the LORD will bestow.
> You will be a crown of splendor in the LORD's hand [*the crown of creation*],
>   a royal diadem in the hand of your God.
> No longer will they call you Deserted,
>   or name your land Desolate.
> But you will be called Hephzibah [*my delight is in her*],

and your land Beulah [*married*];
for the LORD will take delight in you,
and your land will be married.
As a young man marries a maiden [*he pursues her, romances her*] . . .
as a bridegroom rejoices over his bride [*you are lovely*],
so will your God rejoice over you. (Isa. 62:1–5, emphasis added)

"But all who devour you will be devoured;
all your enemies will go into exile.
Those who plunder you will be plundered;
all who make spoil of you I will despoil.
But I will restore you to health and heal your wounds,"
declares the LORD,
"because you are called an outcast,
Zion for whom no one cares." (Jer. 30:16–17)

You really won't understand your life as a woman until you understand this:

You are passionately loved by the God of the universe.
You are passionately hated by his Enemy.

And so, dear heart, it is time for your restoration. For there is One greater than your Enemy. One who has sought you out from the beginning of time. He has come to heal your broken heart and restore your feminine soul. Let us turn now to him.

CHAPTER SIX

Healing the Wound

✿

I didn't know just what was wrong with me,
Till your love helped me name it.
—ARETHA FRANKLIN

Down those old ancient streets,
Down those old ancient roads,
Baby there together we must go
Till we get the healing done.
—VAN MORRISON

Just an hour ago, a hummingbird was trapped in our garage.

They come here to Colorado in the summer, to mate and nest and feast upon the flowers that fill our garden. We love to watch them zipping around, hovering, performing acrobatics in the air. First they go straight up, up, up for thirty feet or so, like a helicopter or like those whirligigs we played with as kids, then plunge straight down as fast as they can, pulling out of a nosedive at the last possible moment to race back up and do it again. Then again. They are playfulness squeezed into a tiny size.

If you get a closer look, these delicate little birds shimmer like emeralds, bright green breasts no bigger than your thumb but glittering like the crown jewels. Others have deep brilliant red throats that glisten in the sun like rubies. They are like living rainbows, flying around our backyard—something out of a fairy tale. Carefree, lovely reminders of God. And then, today, one mistook the open garage door for a new passageway, and once she flew in, she couldn't find her way back out. Poor little thing. She became increasingly panicked as she careened against a window, desperately trying to get back to the world she could see before her, blocked by some invisible shield.

My son Blaine went in to rescue her. His brother Sam's been able to get a few other captives to rest on the end of a long stick, which he then takes out the door and, *whoosh*, off they go into life. But this one panicked even further, making a mad dash across the garage toward another window she perceived as a way out. She crashed against the window at full speed and fell to the floor. Blaine picked her up with a pair of gloves on his hands and took her outside to see if he could revive her. For about fifteen minutes things didn't look good, but then she came back to life and flew away.

What struck me was the compassion and concern we all felt for the rescue of this little jewel. The whole family dropped what we were doing and got involved. (Didn't you feel bad for her as I told her tale?) Now, Jesus said, don't you think God cares just a little bit more for you than for the birds of the air? "Are you not much more valuable than they?" (Matt. 6:26). Indeed, you are. You, dear heart, are the crown of creation, his glorious image bearer. And he will do everything it takes to rescue you and set your heart free.

THE OFFER

Stasi and I lived many years of our Christian life in good churches, churches that taught us the place of worship and sacrifice, faith and suffering, and gave us a love for the Word of God. But in all those years the central ministry of Jesus was never explained to us. We understood, as most Christians do, that Christ came to ransom us from sin and death, to pay the price for our transgressions through his blood shed on the cross so that we might be forgiven, might come home to the Father.

It's true. It's so wonderfully true. Only . . . there is *more*.

The purposes of Jesus Christ are not finished when one of his precious ones is forgiven. Not at all. Would a good father feel satisfied when his daughter is rescued from a car accident, but left in ICU? Doesn't he want her to be healed as well? So God has much more in mind for us. Listen to this passage from Isaiah (it might help to read it very slowly, carefully, out loud to yourself) . . .

> The Spirit of the Sovereign LORD is on me,
> because the LORD has anointed me
> to preach good news to the poor.
> He has sent me to bind up the brokenhearted,
> to proclaim freedom for the captives
> and release from darkness for the prisoners,
> to proclaim the year of the LORD's favor
> and the day of vengeance of our God,
> to comfort all who mourn,
> and provide for those who grieve in Zion—
> to bestow on them a crown of beauty instead of ashes,
> the oil of gladness
> instead of mourning,
> and a garment of praise
> instead of a spirit of despair. (61:1–3)

This is the passage that Jesus pointed to when he began his ministry here on earth. Of all the Scriptures he could have chosen, this is the one he picked on the day he first publicly announced his mission. It must be important to him. It must be central. What does it mean? It's supposed to be really good news, that's clear. It has something to do with healing hearts, setting someone free. Let me try and state it in words more familiar to us.

> God has sent me on a mission.
> I have some great news for you.
> God has sent me to restore and release something.
> And that something is *you.*
> I am here to give you back your heart and set you free.
> I am furious at the Enemy who did this to you, and I will fight against him.
> Let me comfort you.
> For, dear one, I will bestow beauty upon you
> where you have known only devastation.
> Joy, in the places of your deep sorrow.
> And I will robe your heart in thankful praise
> in exchange for your resignation and despair.

Now that is an offer worth considering. What if it were true? I mean, what if Jesus really *could* and *would* do this for your broken heart, your wounded feminine soul? Read it again, and ask him, *Jesus—is this true for me? Would you do this for me?*

He can, and he will . . . if you'll let him.

You are the glorious Image Bearer of the Lord Jesus Christ—the crown of his creation. You have been assaulted. You have fallen to your own resources. Your Enemy has seized upon your wounds and your sins to pin your heart down. Now the Son of God has come to ransom you, *and* to heal your broken, wounded, bleeding heart, *and* to set you free from bondage. He came for the brokenhearted captives. That's me. That's you. He came to *restore* the glorious creation that you are. And then set you free . . . to be yourself.

The LORD their God will save them on that day
as the flock of his people.
They will sparkle in his land
like jewels in a crown.
How attractive and beautiful they will be! (Zech. 9:16–17)

Here is the core reason we wrote this book: to let you know that
the healing of your feminine heart is available, and to help you find
that healing. To help you find the restoration which we long for and
which is central to Jesus' mission. Let him take you by the hand
now and walk with you through your restoration and release.

HEMMED IN

Why did God curse Eve with loneliness and heartache, an emptiness that nothing would be able to fill? Wasn't her life going to be
hard enough out there in the world, banished from the Garden that
was her true home, her only home, never able to return? It seems
unkind. Cruel, even.

He did it to *save* her. For as we all know personally, something
in Eve's heart shifted at the Fall. Something sent its roots down deep
into her soul—and ours—that mistrust of God's heart, that resolu-
tion to find life on our own terms. So God has to thwart her. In
love, he has to block her attempts until, wounded and aching, she
turns to him and him alone for her rescue.

Therefore I will block her path with thornbushes;
I will wall her in so she cannot find her way.
She will chase after her lovers but not catch them;
she will look for them but not find them. (Hos. 2:6–7)

Jesus has to thwart us too—thwart our self-redemptive plans, our controlling and our hiding, thwart the ways we are seeking to fill the ache within us. Otherwise, we would never fully turn to him for our rescue. Oh, we might turn to him for our "salvation," for a ticket to heaven when we die. We might turn to him even in the form of Christian service, regular church attendance, a moral life. But *inside*, our hearts remain broken and captive and far from the One who can help us.

And so you will see the gentle, firm hand of God in a woman's life hemming her in. He'll make what once was a great job miserable, if it was in her career that she found shelter. He'll bring hardship into her marriage, even to the breaking point, if it was in marriage she sought her salvation. Wherever it is we have sought life apart from him, he disrupts our plans, our "way of life" that is not life at all. Listen to Susan's story:

> Things at work have been hard. It caused me to go to my posture of defensiveness. I wanted to say, "You don't understand—you don't know my story. I have to defend myself because no one else will." I grew up with an alcoholic father and a mother who suffers extreme emotional problems. At a very young age (8 or so) I became the one who when my father beat my mother would step in to defend her, and when my mother would berate my father I was the one who would step in to defend him. Up until I was 16 I took all the verbal abuse my mother had thrown at me, but there was this day that I decided not to take it anymore. My father told me I needed to go back in there and take it. This arrow pierced my heart so deeply that the walls of my heart became impenetrable. I've not allowed this wound to be touched for many, many years.
>
> God has shown me that because of the defensiveness I buried my truly feminine heart which longs so deeply to be pursued and fought for, to be seen as beautiful, to be tender and

kind, to feel deeply. He has shown me that by bringing this into my marriage, I have not allowed Dave the opportunity to fight for me. For this I am grieved. God asked me to repent of this to Dave and take the risk of being vulnerable once again. I stand now in this risky place of vulnerability, with a bleeding heart waiting and praying. Every day I must choose to lay down my defensiveness and allow the healing balm of Jesus to attend to my wound and allow him to be my God, my Strength, and my Defender.

He told me that I didn't need to defend myself anymore, that was his job, he is my Defender and Advocate. Would I let him be that for me? I said yes. There was a huge weight lifted off that I can't fully explain.

TURNING FROM THE WAYS YOU'VE
SOUGHT TO SAVE YOURSELF

Change a few of the details and you have my story—and yours. We construct a life of safety (I will not be vulnerable *there*) and find some place to get a taste of being enjoyed or at least of being "needed." Our journey toward healing begins when we repent of those ways, lay them down, let them go. They've been a royal disaster anyway. As Frederick Buechner says,

> To do for yourself the best that you have it in you to do—to grit your teeth and clench your fists in order to survive the world at its harshest and worst—is, by that very act, to be unable to let something be done for you and in you that is more wonderful still. The trouble with steeling yourself against the harshness of reality is that the same steel that secures your life against being destroyed secures your life also against being opened up and transformed. (*The Sacred Journey*)

God comes to us and asks, *Will you let me come for you?* Not only does he thwart, but at the same time he calls to us as he did to our friend Susan, *Set it down. Set it down. Turn from your ways to me. I want to come for you.*

> Therefore I am now going to allure her;
> I will lead her into the desert
> and speak tenderly to her. (Hos. 2:14)

To enter the journey toward the healing of your feminine heart, all it requires is a, *Yes. Okay.* A simple turning in the heart. Like the Prodigal we wake one day to see that the life we've constructed is no life at all. We let desire speak to us again; we let our hearts have a voice, and what the voice usually says is, *This isn't working. My life is a disaster. Jesus—I'm sorry. Forgive me. Please come for me.* So begin here, pray just this:

> *Jesus, I give myself to you. I give my life to you. I surrender me—totally and completely. Forgive all my sins, my hurtful ways. Forgive all my self-protecting and all of my chasing after other comforters. Come for me now, dear Lord. Come and be my Savior, my Healer, my Love.*

INVITE HIM IN

There is a famous passage of Scripture that many people have heard in the context of an invitation to know Christ as Savior. "Behold, I stand at the door and knock. If anyone hears My voice and opens the door, I will come in" (Rev. 3:20 NKJV). He does not force himself upon us. He knocks, and waits for us to ask him in. There is an initial step, the first step of this, which we call salvation. We hear Christ knocking and we open our hearts to him as Savior. It is the first turning. But the principle of this "knocking and waiting for permission to come in" remains true well into our Christian life.

You see, we all pretty much handle our brokenness in the same way—we mishandle it. It hurts too much to go there. So we shut the door to that room in our hearts, and we throw away the key— much like Lord Craven locks the Secret Garden upon the death of his wife and buries the key. But that does not bring healing. Not at all. It might bring relief—for a while. But never healing. Usually it orphans the little girl in that room, leaves her to fend for herself. The best thing we can do is to let Jesus come in; open the door and invite him in to find us in those hurting places.

It might come as a surprise that Christ asks our permission to come in and heal, but he is kind, and the door is shut from the inside, and healing never comes *against* our will. In order to experience his healing, we must also give him permission to come in to the places we have so long shut to anyone. *Will you let me heal you?* He knocks through our loneliness. He knocks through our sorrows. He knocks through events that feel too close to what happened to us when we were young—a betrayal, a rejection, a word spoken, a relationship lost. He knocks through many things, waiting for us to give him permission to enter in.

Give him permission. Give him access to your broken heart. Ask him to come to *these* places.

Yes, Jesus, yes. I do invite you in. Come to my heart in these shattered places. [You know what they are—ask him there. Is it the abuse? The loss of your father? The jealousy of your mother? Ask him in.] *Come to me, my Savior. I open this door of my heart. I give you permission to heal my wounds. Come to me here. Come for me here.*

RENOUNCE THE AGREEMENTS YOU'VE MADE

Your wounds brought messages with them. Lots of messages. Somehow they all usually land in the same place. They had a similar

theme. "You're worthless." "You're not a woman." "You're too much
. . . and not enough." "You're a disappointment." "You are repulsive."
On and on they go. Because they were delivered with such pain, they
felt true. They pierced our hearts, and they seemed so true. So we
accepted the messages as fact. We embraced them as the verdict on us.

As we said earlier, the vows we made as children act like a deep-
seated agreement with the messages of our wounds. "Fine. If that's
how it is, then that's how it is. I'll live my life in the following way
. . ." The vows we made acted like a kind of covenant with the messages that came with our deep wounds. Those childhood vows are
very dangerous things. We must renounce them. *Before* we are
entirely convinced that they aren't true, we must reject the messages
of our wounds. It's a way of unlocking the door to Jesus.
Agreements lock the door from the inside. Renouncing the agreements unlocks the door to him.

*Jesus, forgive me for embracing these lies. This is not what you have
said of me. You said I am your daughter, your beloved, your cherished
one. I renounce the agreements I made with* [name the specific
messages you've been living with. "I'm stupid. I'm ugly." You
know what they are.] *I renounce the agreements I've been making
with these messages all these years. Bring the truth here, oh Spirit of
Truth. I reject these lies.*

WE FIND OUR TEARS

Part of the reason women are so tired is because we are spending *so*
much energy trying to "keep it together." So much energy devoted
to suppressing the pain and keeping a good appearance. "I'm gonna
harden my heart," sang Rindy Ross. "I'm gonna swallow my tears."
A terrible, costly way to live your life. Part of this is driven by fear
that the pain will overwhelm us. That we will be consumed by our

sorrow. It's an understandable fear—but it is no more true than the fear we had of the dark as children. Grief, dear sisters, is good. Grief helps to heal our hearts. Why, Jesus himself was a "Man of sorrows and acquainted with grief" (Isa. 53:3 NKJV).

Let the tears come. Get alone, get to your car or your bedroom or the shower and let the tears come. Let the tears come. It is the only kind thing to do for your woundedness. Allow yourself to feel again. And feel you will—many things. Anger. That's okay. Anger's not a sin (Eph. 4:26). Remorse. Of course you feel remorse and regret for so many lost years. Fear. Yes, that makes sense. Jesus can handle the fear as well. In fact, there is no emotion you can bring up that Jesus can't handle. (Look at the psalms—they are a raging sea of emotions.)

Let it all out.

As Augustine wrote in his *Confessions*, "The tears . . . streamed down, and I let them flow as freely as they would, making of them a pillow for my heart. On them it rested." Grief is a form of validation; it says the wound *mattered*. It mattered. You mattered. That's not the way life was supposed to go. There are unwept tears down in there—the tears of a little girl who is lost and frightened. The tears of a teenage girl who's been rejected and has no place to turn. The tears of a woman whose life has been hard and lonely and nothing close to her dreams.

Let the tears come.

FORGIVE

Okay—now for a hard step (as if the others have been easy). A real step of courage and will. We must forgive those who hurt us. The reason is simple: Bitterness and unforgiveness set their hooks deep in our hearts; they are chains that hold us captive to the wounds and the messages of those wounds. Until you forgive, you remain their prisoner. Paul warns us that unforgiveness and bitterness can wreck our lives and the lives of others (Eph. 4:31; Heb. 12:15). We have to let it all go.

> Forgive as the Lord forgave you. (Col. 3:13)

Now—listen carefully. Forgiveness is a *choice*. It is not a feeling—don't try and feel forgiving. It is an act of the will. "Don't wait to forgive until you feel like forgiving," wrote Neil Anderson. "You will never get there. Feelings take time to heal after the choice to forgive is made." We allow God to bring the hurt up from our past, for "if your forgiveness doesn't visit the emotional core of your life, it will be incomplete," said Anderson. We acknowledge that it hurt, that it mattered, and we choose to extend forgiveness to our fathers, our mothers, those who hurt us. This is *not* saying, "It didn't really matter"; it is *not* saying, "I probably deserved part of it anyway." Forgiveness says, "It was wrong. Very wrong. It mattered, hurt me deeply. And I release you. I give you to God. I will not be your captive here any longer."

It might help to remember that those who hurt you were also deeply wounded themselves. They were broken hearts, broken when they were young, and they fell captive to the Enemy. They were in fact pawns in his hands. This doesn't absolve them of the choices they made, the things they did. It just helps us to let them go—to realize that they were shattered souls themselves, used by our true Enemy in his war against femininity.

ASK JESUS TO HEAL YOU

We turn from our self-redemptive strategies. We open the door of our hurting heart to Jesus. We renounce the agreements we made with the messages of our wounds, renounce any vows we made. We forgive those who harmed us. And then, with an open heart, we simply ask Jesus to heal us. Melissa was the young girl who "vowed I would be tough; hard, like a rock," and became so for many years. But that is not the end of her story. She came to the place where Jesus asked to heal her wounded heart. She gave him permission to come in. This is what happened.

God went back and got the shaking little girl that was hiding under the bed and convinced her to come out. He unclenched her little fists and took her hand and placed it in his and answered her question. He held her and told her it was OK for her not to be tough. He would protect her. She didn't have to be strong. He told her she wasn't a rock but a child. An innocent child. His child. He didn't condemn her for anything but instead understood her and loved her! He told her she was special . . . like no other and that she had special gifts like no other. She knew his voice and trusted him. She could hear the pleasure he had for her in his voice and felt his delight in her as he talked. He was so gentle and loving she couldn't help but melt in his arms.

This is available. This is the offer of our Savior—to heal our broken hearts. To come to the young places within us and find us there, take us in his arms, bring us home. The time has come to let Jesus heal you.

Jesus, come to me and heal my heart. Come to the shattered places within me. Come for the little girl that was wounded. Come and hold me in your arms, and heal me. Do for me what you promised to do— heal my broken heart and set me free.

ASK HIM TO DESTROY YOUR ENEMIES

In the beautiful passage of Isaiah 61, God promises "freedom for the captives and release from darkness for the prisoners" (v. 1). He goes on to proclaim "vengeance" against our enemies (v. 2). Our wounds, our vows, and the agreements we've made with the messages all give ground to the Enemy in our lives. Paul warns about this in Ephesians 4 when he says—writing to Christians—"and do not give the devil a foothold" (v. 27). There are things you've struggled with all your life—self-doubt, anger, depression, shame, addiction, fear. You probably thought that those were your fault too.

But they are not. They came from the Enemy who wanted to take your heart captive, make you a prisoner of darkness. To be sure, we complied. We allowed those strongholds to form when we mishandled our wounds and made those vows. But Jesus has forgiven us for all of that, and now he wants to set us free.

Ask him to destroy your enemies. He promised to, after all. Ask Jesus to release your heart from captivity to these things.

Jesus, come and rescue me. Set me free from [you know what you need freedom from—name it]. *Release me from darkness. Bring your vengeance on my enemies. I reject them and ask you to take them to judgment. Set my heart free.*

LET HIM FATHER YOU

Then he went with Sara into her little sitting room and they bade each other good-bye. Sara sat on his knee and held the lapels of his coat in her small hands and looked long and hard at his face.

"Are you learning me by heart, little Sara?" he said, stroking her hair.

"No," she answered. "I know you by heart. You are inside my heart." And they put their arms round each other and kissed as if they would never let each other go. (Frances Hodgson Burnett, *A Little Princess*)

This precious story touches something deep in the hearts of little girls—and women. Every little girl was made to live in a world with a father who loves her unconditionally. She first learns who God is, what he is like, and how he feels about her from her earthly dad. God is "Our Father, who art in heaven." He means initially to reveal himself to his daughters and his sons through the love of our dads. We were meant to know a father's love, be kept safe in it, be protected by it, and blossom there.

I (Stasi) have heard many times that what we at first believe about God, the Father, directly comes from what we know of and have experienced from our earthly dads. I first heard this from a pulpit as a young Christian and in my typical, teachable fashion, thought, *How stupid.* Not that the pastor was stupid, but that the idea itself was ludicrous. Of course, my own dad was not God. Everybody knew that. But later, as I heard other women speak of God the Father, I often heard in their voices a softness, a tenderness, perhaps even a childlikeness that was foreign to me. When I began to hear others praying to "Daddy" or "Papa," I knew they were speaking to "Someone" I did not know.

I had never called my own father "Daddy." "Papa" was what fathers were called in movies. Many of us grew up in homes where the correct term for Dad was "Sir." Intimacy with and dependence on a father who was rarely home—and emotionally absent when he was—was impossible for me. Remember—he didn't want to know me. I was a disappointment to him.

I have come to understand that what that pastor was telling me so many years ago was the truth. I was looking at my heavenly Father through the lenses of my experiences with my own father. And for me, that meant my heavenly Father was distant, aloof, unavailable, hard to please, easily disappointed, quick to anger, and often hard to predict. True, I wanted to please him. But since God the Father was, to me, hard to fathom and not especially inviting, my relationship with God centered on my relationship with his Son. Jesus liked me. I wasn't so sure about his dad.

Years into my Christian life, I began to hunger to know God more deeply as my Father. I asked him to reveal himself to me as my dad. In answer, God invited me to take a journey deep into my heart that took surprising turns and continues still. First, God led me into taking a much closer look at my own father. Who was he really? How did he really feel about me? What did I even remember? God invited me to go with him into the deep places of my heart that were hidden and wounded and bleeding still from heartbreaks and wounds I had received from my father's hand. Places I did not want to go. Memories I did not want to revisit. Emotions I did not want to feel. The only reason I said yes to God, the only reason I would travel there, was because I knew he would go with me. Hand in hand. He would hold my heart. And I had come to trust his.

There is a core part of our hearts that was made for Daddy. Made for his strong and tender love. That part is still there, and longing. Open it to Jesus and to your Father God. Ask him to come and love you there. Meet you there. We've all tried so hard to find the fulfillment of this love in other people, and it never, ever works. Let us give this treasure back to the One who can love us best.

Father, I need your love. Come to the core of my heart. Come and bring your love for me. Help me to know you for who you really are—not as I see my earthly father. Reveal yourself to me. Reveal your love for me. Tell me what I mean to you. Come, and father me.

ASK HIM TO ANSWER YOUR QUESTION

Those of you who have read *A Little Princess* by Frances Hodgson Burnett will recall that life did not go well for Sara. In the middle of her eleventh birthday party, word reaches the school that her beloved Papa has died. His fortune has been confiscated, and she is penniless. With no means to pay for her private education, Sara is demeaned, put to work, treated cruelly, and sent to live in the barren attic.

But the love Sara's father poured into her heart has made a lasting impact. Poor, bereft, and ill treated, Sara has a heart of gold. She says to herself, "Whatever comes, cannot alter one thing. If I am a princess in rags and tatters, I can be a princess inside. It would be easy to be a princess if I were dressed in a cloth of gold, but it is a great deal more of a triumph to be one all the time when no one knows it."

How do you come to such a confidence? You take your heart's deepest Question to God. You still have a Question, dear one. We all do. We all still need to know, *Do you see me? Am I captivating? Do I have a beauty all my own?*

I realized last year that this question still needed an answer in Stasi's own heart. We were out to dinner for our anniversary. At one point in the evening I said, "You were a darling little girl." She looked at me with a sort of *Don't lie to me* kind of look. "Didn't you know that?" A long pause. "No." "Oh, sweetheart—you didn't *know?*" I have seen the photos. I have seen glimpses into what a treasure she was. But life wrote a different message on her heart. And so I urged her, "You must ask God what he saw. Take this to him."

We could tell you so many beautiful stories of women who have received from God the answer to their Question. As a young girl our friend Kim longed to be the princess who was being rescued during childhood games. "But the girl down the street was cuter than me. She was Barbie. So I had to join on the side of the guys, fight the dragon, and rescue her. I never got to be the Beauty." Tears came with this story—young tears, tears than had never been cried over this. It was good to finally let them out. "Kim, I tell you what I want you to do. I want you to ask Jesus to show you your beauty." "I can do that?" she said. "I mean, that's okay? He would do that for me?"

She came back after two months, smiling as if she had some great secret to tell. Her face was shining. She told us that Jesus had come. He had shown her beauty—her own—in lots of ways. More than two hundred ways. "It's been amazing. I'm beginning to believe I'm beautiful."

Just a few weeks ago I was talking with our friend Debbie; she's the one whose father had an affair and who has spent so much time and energy trying to "fix" whatever was wrong with her. "What if you have a genuine and captivating beauty that is marred only by your striving?" She leaned back against her chair and sighed at the thought. Something softened. Suddenly she was soft and beautiful. The veil was parted, and there she was—a beautiful woman. Gone was the resignation; gone were the anxiety and pain. She was, for a moment, at rest. "What does your heart do with that possibility?" A moment's pause. "Two things arise in me," she said. " 'Hooray!' and, 'Damn!' " I smiled at her honesty. "*Hooray* that it might be true after all, and *damn* because what have I been doing all these years?"

Let's just start with a thought. What if the message delivered with your wounds simply isn't true about you? Let that sink in. It wasn't true. What does it free you to do? Weep? Rejoice? Let go? Come out? Take your heart back? Here is one woman's experience:

Even though I've "succeeded" in many areas, I've always been ashamed of the absence of my femininity as defined by the world. Asking God what he thought of me as a woman was beyond agonizing. I wrestled with him right to the end. I knew in my mind he wouldn't be mean, but I was convinced I had failed him miserably in this department . . . When I finally allowed myself to hear God speak a new name, it was Grace. And the lie of "too much boy and not enough girl" gets shattered in a moment. He crowns me with Grace, He crowns me with love. And I'm satisfied (Ps. 103).

A DEEPER HEALING

I am rereading this book today after five years and thanking God for it; gleaning more from it for myself! And I want to encourage you that healing truly is available. A deeper healing has occurred in my heart in the past year than I even knew was possible.

I've written about the effect of my father's disengagement, his brokenness, his sin upon my life. I want to tell you now about what was more true: his engagement, his concern, his love. In seeking God and his eyes on my life, my identity, and my heart, God is revealing to me a life story that is different than the one I have remembered for the majority of my life. I turned fifty years old this year and God continues to do amazing things.

I still remember the old stories of what happened. But the sting of death has been removed from the memories. They no longer hurt. There are not tears to be shed over them any more. The pain is gone. Things happened. Yes. But God is reminding me that other things happened as well. He is bringing to my mind memories and experiences long forgotten. Sweet memories. Good experiences. He is telling me my story afresh and it is a good one.

My mother was overwhelmed with the prospect of another child. My father was delighted. Returning from his many business trips, he often brought us, his children, little presents. A stuffed animal. A toy. A huge balloon! As the youngest in the family, he sometimes gave me special things—one Christmas it was a plastic blow-up Rudolph. As a teenager, there were two times when I came home from school to find a new outfit on my bed. From my dad.

One year I was going with friends skiing for the first time and came home prior to the trip to find a red snow jacket on my bed. It is hanging in my closet now. Outdated. Old. Precious to me.

My father loved me. He wanted me. So truly did my mother. The answer to the Question of my little girl's heart, "Am I lovely? Do you delight in me?" was a resounding *yes*. It was a yes from my earthly parents, and it is a yes from my heavenly Father. God has rewritten my personal history. There is a lightness to my heart that is new. A deeper joy is residing there as I embrace ever more fully the love of my God and what he speaks to me about myself and life.

It is amazing. It is available. Keep pressing in. Keep asking God.

And take your heart's Question to Jesus. Ask him to show you your beauty. And then? Let him Romance you.

CHAPTER SEVEN

Romance∂

✿

I have loved you with an everlasting love.
—GOD (JEREMIAH 31:3)

Romance is the deepest thing in life.
It is deeper even than reality.
—G. K. CHESTERTON

*I*t had been a long, busy day, and I left the boys with John and escaped into the night for some much-needed time alone. It was a beautiful fall Colorado night. I walked along a path toward a park near our home. The air was crisp and clear, the stars winking, glistening. I breathed in the beauty and laid the cares of the day behind me. A cool breeze whispered by, one of the first to speak of the winter to come. As I walked, I was dazzled by the splendor of it all, and I began to compliment God on the great job he had done. "It's beautiful, Lord! The stars are amazing!"

I'm glad you like it, my darling.

I stopped dead in my tracks. I blushed. Did the God of the universe just call me "darling"? Was that *okay?* I was warmed to the depths of my soul by the endearment, but I also wondered if I had made it up. And was it sacrilegious to believe God would use such a loving name? For me? I am the one who had lost patience with her children that very day and used an ugly tone of voice that hurt them and mortified me. I am the one who is living her life so imperfectly, disappointing friends and failing family.

Me? *Darling?*

Later that night I began to read some Scriptures before falling asleep, and my hand turned to the pages of the Song of Songs. My eyes fell to the words "How beautiful you are, my darling" (1:15). How kind of God, for then I knew. It had been him. The amazing love of God for *me* penetrated my heart in a new and deep way that night. He had spoken to me. This wild God of mine, who knows my every thought and intention, who sees my every failure and sin, loves me. Not in a religious way, not in the way we usually translate when we hear, "God loves us." Which usually sounds like "because he has to" or meaning "he tolerates you." No. He loves me as a *Lover* loves. Whoa.

LONGING FOR ROMANCE

A woman becomes beautiful when she knows she's loved. We've seen this many times—you probably have too. Cut off from love, rejected, no one pursuing her, something in a woman wilts like a flower no one waters anymore. She withers into resignation, duty, and shame. The radiance of her countenance goes out, as if a light has been turned off. But this same woman, whom everyone thought was rather plain and unengaging, becomes lovely and inviting when she is *pursued*. Her heart begins to come alive, come to the surface, and her countenance becomes radiant. We wonder, *Where has she been all these years? Why, she really is captivating.*

Think of Fran in *Strictly Ballroom*, or Tulah in *My Big Fat Greek Wedding*. Remember Lottie in *Enchanted April*, Adrian in *Rocky*, or Danielle in *Ever After*. Their beauty was always there. What happened to each woman was merely the power of romance *releasing* her true beauty, awakening her heart. She has come alive. As women we long to be loved in a certain way, a way unique to our femininity. We long for romance. We are wired for it; it's what makes our hearts come alive. You know that. Somewhere, down deep inside, you know this. But what you might never have known is this . . .

This doesn't need to wait for a man. ←

God longs to bring this into your life himself. He wants you to move beyond the childlike "Jesus loves me, this I know, for the Bible tells me so." He wants to heal us through his love to become mature women who actually *know* him. He wants us to *experience* verses like, "Therefore I am now going to allure her; I will lead her into the desert and speak tenderly to her" (Hos. 2:14). And "You have stolen my heart, my sister, my bride" (Song 4:9). Our hearts are desperate for this. What would it be like to experience for yourself that the truest thing about his heart toward yours is not disappointment or disapproval but deep, fiery, passionate love? This is, after all, what a woman was made for.

Faithful obedience to God is vital, but it is not all God draws us to. It is not sufficient for our healing, no more than doing the laundry is sufficient for a marriage. And it will not be enough in the long run to carry us through. The persecuted Church is vast today. More Christians are being martyred in our lifetime than in *any* other time in church history. It is not obedience that is carrying our brothers and sisters—unwavering, steadfast, eyes ablaze—to their deaths. It is holy, fierce *passion*. Hearts afire.

For the root of all holiness is Romance.

GOD AS LOVER

Let's go back for a moment to the movies that you love. Think of one of the most romantic scenes you can remember, scenes that made you sigh. Jack with Rose on the bow of the *Titanic*, his arms around her waist, their first kiss. Wallace speaking in French to Murron, then in Italian: "Not as beautiful as you." Aragorn, standing with Arwen in the moonlight on the bridge in Rivendell, declaring his love for her. Edward returning for Elinor in *Sense and Sensibility,* and Professor Behr returning for Jo at the end of *Little Women.*

Now, put yourself in the scene as the Beauty, and Jesus as the Lover.

What does your heart do with that? Is there a bit of a hesitation, "Is that okay?" Is there a bit of longing, "I'd love for that to happen"? Perhaps there might be for some of you a tinge of fear, the wince of your wounded heart, "I don't want to open that up." Then you can see that there is healing for your heart in moving toward this. It's okay. It's quite biblical. Jesus calls himself the Bridegroom (Matt. 9:15; Matt. 25:1–10; John 3:29). Now, you'll need to take the religious drapery and sanctimonious gilding off of this. *Bridegroom* simply means fiancé. Lover. This is the most intimate of all the metaphors Jesus chose to describe his love and longing for us, and the kind of relationship he invites us into.

You might recall that the Scriptures use a number of metaphors to describe our relationship with God. We are portrayed as clay, and he is the potter. We are sheep, and he the shepherd. Each metaphor is beautiful and speaks to the various seasons of our spiritual lives and to the various aspects of God's heart toward us. But have you noticed they *ascend* in a stunning way? From potter and his clay to a shepherd and his sheep, there is a marked difference in intimacy, in the way they relate. It gets even better. From master and servant to father and child, there is a wonderful progression into greater intimacy. It grows more beautiful and rich when he calls us his friends. But what is most breathtaking is when God says he is our Lover (our Bridegroom, our Fiancé), and we his bride. That is the pinnacle, the goal of our redemption (used in the last chapter of the

Bible, when Christ returns for his bride) and the most intimate and romantic of all.

If you'll open your heart to the possibility, you'll find that God has been wooing you ever since you were a little girl. Yes, we said earlier that the story of your life is the story of the long and sustained assault upon your heart by the one who knows what you could be and fears you. But that is only *part* of the story. Every story has a villain. Every story also has a hero. The Great Love Story the Scriptures are telling us about also reveals a Lover who longs for you. The story of your life is *also* the story of the long and passionate pursuit of your heart by the One who knows you best and loves you most.

God has written the Romance not only on our hearts but all over the world around us. What we need is for him to open our eyes, to open our ears that we might recognize his voice calling to us, see his hand wooing us in the beauty that quickens our hearts.

> *Longer than there've been fishes in the ocean*
> *Higher than any bird ever flew*
> *Longer than there've been stars up in the heavens*
> *I've been in love with you.*
>
> *Stronger than any mountain cathedral*
> *Truer than any tree ever grew*
> *Deeper than any forest primeval*
> *I am in love with you.*
> —DAN FOGELBERG, "LONGER"

What were the things that romanced your heart as a girl? Was it horses in a field? Was it the fragrance of the air after a summer rain? Was it a favorite book like *The Secret Garden*? The first snowfall of winter? Those were all whispers from your Lover, notes sent to awaken your heart's longings. And as we journey into a true intimacy with God as women, he often brings those things back into our lives, to remind us he *was* there, to heal and restore things that were lost or stolen.

OPENING OUR HEARTS TO THE ROMANCER

Every song you love, every memory you cherish, every moment that has moved you to holy tears has been given to you from the One who has been pursuing you from your first breath in order to win your heart. God's version of flowers and chocolates and candlelight dinners comes in the form of sunsets and falling stars, moonlight on lakes and cricket symphonies; warm wind, swaying trees, lush gardens, and fierce devotion.

This romancing is immensely personal. It will be as if it has been scripted for *your* heart. He knows what takes your breath away, knows what makes your heart beat faster. We have missed many of his notes simply because we shut our hearts down in order to endure the pain of life. Now, in our healing journey as women, we must open our hearts again, and keep them open. Not foolishly, not to anyone and anything. But yes, we must choose to open our hearts again so that we might hear his whispers, receive his kisses.

It may not come the way we thought, or perhaps even thought we desired it to. A few years ago John was on a business trip to Oregon. He snuck away for some time alone with God, down to the beach where he walked and prayed and finally sat in the sand to watch the waves upon the sea. (His idea of refreshment is "the wilder the better.") Then he saw it. A huge plume of water shot up into the sky, and a massive humpback whale appeared right before him, impossibly close to shore. No one else was near. The time of the whale's annual migration had long passed. John knew immediately that this was a gift from God to his heart alone, a gift from the Lover of his heart.

John told me this story, and as happy as I was for him, I was more hungry for such a kiss for myself. I wanted a whale too. I wanted to experience God's love for me, personally. It wasn't long after this that John and I were in northern California speaking at a couples' retreat. I, too, snuck away one morning for some much needed time on the beach with God. I sat on the sand, looked out to the sea, and asked God for a whale. "I know you love John, Jesus, but do you love me too? That much? If you do, may I have a whale too?"

I felt a little silly in asking, for I knew the truth—that God had already proven his love for me. He had sent his only Son, Jesus, to die for me (John 3:16). He had rescued me. He had paid the highest price imaginable for me. He had given me all of creation to speak of his great glory and love, and he had given me the Word of God in all its depth and beauty, and here I was, asking for more. And God loved it. God delights in revealing himself to those who will seek him with all their hearts. He is an extravagant, abundant Lover, and he loves to reveal his heart to us again and again.

After a while, with no whale in sight, I got up off the sand and continued to walk. It was early spring, waves crashing, seagulls crying. The northern coast of California is rocky, and as I picked my way through, I rounded a corner and came upon a starfish, a beautiful orange starfish. And I knew at once it was God's gift to me, his kiss. He didn't give me a whale; no, that was for John alone. For me, unique to me, he gave a stunning starfish. He answered my question. Yes. He loved me. I thanked him for it, then rounded the next bend and came upon a sight I will never forget. There before me, behind me, surrounding me, were hundreds of starfish. Zillions of them. There were purple ones and orange ones and blue ones, all sizes. I burst into joyful laughter, my heart exploding inside me.

God didn't just love me. He LOOOOVED me! Intimately, personally, completely.

God gave John a whale. It was huge and strong. God gave me starfish. They were delicate, small, intricate. I could touch them. In being surrounded by them, I felt my heart encompassed by his generous, extravagant love. The amazing starfish were an intimate gift from an intimate God. He has many for you as well. Perhaps it would be good to ask,

Jesus, how are you romancing me now?

We don't always see it. In chapter 1 we told you of the romantic ball we attended a few years ago. Leslie, a dear friend of ours, was also invited. But she almost missed the invitation. The story is amazing. Several weeks before she received her invitation she had said to God, "I am tired of living in the cellar. I want to come out. I want to go to the ball." She knew nothing of what was in store, knew nothing of the planned ball—she was simply letting her heart express itself in vulnerability to God. She felt like Cinderella in the cellar. And she wanted *out*. (He loves your vulnerability, as any Lover does. He loves it when you share your truest heart's desire with him.) Well, when she got the invitation, she didn't even open it. It sat for a few weeks in the bills pile.

And when she finally did open it—a lovely embossed invitation to a real ball—she didn't think it was for her. Oh, Cinderella. What will it take? A few days later God opened her eyes, and she ran back to the mail, pulled out the invitation, and held her breath. "Really, God? This is really true?" She didn't want to arrange. She waited for her husband to ask her if she'd like to go. He did. The evening was, for her, a deeply healing event, reaching back and addressing old wounds. She was lit up all night, and something has remained lit ever since.

This is not to say that life is one big romantic moment with Jesus. I live a life much like yours—full of demands, pressures, and disappointments. Right now the laundry is going, all the dishes are dirty, there's no food for lunch, and the boys are bored with summer vacation. Like you, there are seasons in my life when Jesus seems very near and seasons where I can't seem to find him at all. Sometimes it feels like we're playing a game of hide-and-seek, but he's got all the best hiding places staked out. All relationships ebb and flow.

The ebbing is to draw our hearts out in deeper longing. In the times of emptiness, an open heart *notices*. What are you feeling? Like a lonely girl missing her daddy? Like a teenage young woman feeling completely invisible, unseen? Often God allows these feelings to surface to help us go back to times when we have felt like this before. Notice also what you want to do—how you handle your heart. Are you shutting down in anger? Turning to food? To others?

What is crucial is that *this* time we handle our hearts differently. We ask our Lover to come for us, and we keep our eyes and our hearts open to his coming. We choose not to shut down. We let the tears come. We allow the ache to swell into a longing prayer for our God. And he comes, dear hearts. He does come. The times of intimacy—the flowing waters of love—those times then bring healing to places in our hearts that still need his touch.

WHAT DOES GOD WANT FROM YOU?

I am searching through the canyon.
It is your name that I am calling.
Though you're so far away
I know you hear my plea
Why won't you answer me?

Here I am.

Here I am.

—EMMYLOU HARRIS, "HERE I AM"

I was walking through the music store the other day, just sort of browsing, not really after anything in particular, and I sensed the Spirit say, *Buy this CD.* Just a nudge, not a shout, but I bought it and plugged it into my player on the way home. I wasn't really moved by it. I gave it to Stasi, who came back and told me how incredible it was. She played the song for me, and I "heard" it for what it was. The Romancer calling once again. He has done this for us more times than we could ever count—songs, movies, cards, words from friends, moments in the woods—the Romance is *everywhere.* It is your name that he is calling.

What is it that God wants from you?

He wants the same thing that you want. He wants to be loved. He wants to be known as only lovers can know each other. He wants intimacy with you. Yes, yes, he wants your obedience, but only when it flows out of a heart filled with love for him. "Whoever has my commands and obeys them, he is the one who loves me" (John 14:21). Following hard after Jesus is the heart's natural response when it has been captured and has fallen deeply in love with him.

Reading George MacDonald several years ago, I came across an astounding thought. You've probably heard that there is in every human heart a place that God alone can fill. (Lord knows we've tried to fill it with everything else, to our utter dismay.) But what the old poet was saying was that there is *also* in God's heart a place that you alone can fill. "It follows that there is also a chamber in God himself, into which none can enter but the one, the individual." You. You are meant to fill a place in the heart of God no one and nothing else can fill. Whoa. He longs for *you.*

You are the one that overwhelms his heart with just "one glance of your eyes" (Song 4:9b). You are the one he sings over with delight and longs to dance with across mountaintops and ballroom floors (Zeph. 3:17). You are the one who takes his breath away by your beautiful heart that, against all odds, hopes in him. Let that be true for a moment. Let it be true of *you*.

God wants to live this life together with you, to share in your days and decisions, your desires and disappointments. He wants intimacy with you in the midst of the madness and mundane, the meetings and memos, the laundry and lists, the carpools and conversations and projects and pain. He wants to pour his love into your heart, and he longs to have you pour yours into his. He wants your deep heart, that center place within that is the truest *you*. He is not interested in intimacy with the woman you think you are supposed to be. He wants intimacy with the real you.

Here's how the flow goes in Hosea. First, God says that he will thwart our efforts to find life apart from him (we quoted this part earlier).

> Therefore I will block her path with thornbushes;
> I will wall her in so that she cannot find her way.
> She will chase after her lovers but not catch them;
> she will look for them but not find them. (2:6–7)

He does this, as we said, in order to wear us out, get us to turn back to him in thirsty longing. Then he begins to woo us. He often takes us aside from every other source of comfort so that he alone can have our heart's attention.

> Therefore I am now going to allure her;
> I will lead her into the desert
> and speak tenderly to her. (2:14)

And it is here that we begin to experience him not as the God-way-up-there, not the God-of-Sunday-mornings, but as the pursuer of our hearts. As Lover.

> "In that day," declares the LORD,
> "you will call me 'my husband';
> you will no longer call me 'my master . . .'
>
> I will betroth you to me forever;
> I will betroth you in righteousness and justice,
> in love and compassion." (2:16, 19)

In the spacious love of God, our souls can lie down and rest. This love from him is not something we must struggle for, earn, or fear to lose. It is bestowed. He has bestowed it upon us. He has chosen us. And nothing can separate us from his love. Not even we, ourselves. We are made for such a love. Our hearts yearn to be loved intimately, personally, and yes, romantically. We are created to be the object of desire and affection of one who is totally and completely in love with us.

And we are.

An intimate relationship with Jesus is not only for other women, for women who seem to have their acts together, who appear godly and whose nails are nicely shaped. It is for each and every one of us. God wants intimacy with *you*. In order to have it, you, too, must offer it to him.

ADORING HEARTS

As Jesus and his disciples were on their way, he came to a village where a woman named Martha opened her home to him. She had a sister called Mary, who sat at the Lord's feet listening to what he said. But Martha was distracted by all the preparations that had to be made. She came to him and asked, "Lord, don't you care that my sister has left me to do the work by myself? Tell her to help me!"

"Martha, Martha," the Lord answered, "you are worried and upset about many things, but only one thing is needed. Mary has chosen what is better, and it will not be taken away from her." (Luke 10:38–42)

Okay, we've all heard the story. Martha and Mary. Don't be such a Martha. Got it. But we've often wondered what the "one thing" was that was needed. Some of you might have heard teaching that it was one simple casserole dish, that Martha was busy making a complicated meal when only one simple food was needed. No. That is not what Jesus is saying. Jesus has again spoken straight into the heart of the matter. The one thing that is needed is a captivated, adoring heart, a heart that *responds* to the extravagant love of God with worship.

Our hearts are made to worship. It is what we do; we can't help it. Now, worship is one of those words made sickly by religion. We hear "worship" and we think, *She's talking about going to church. Singing hymns.* Nope. Worship is far more passionate, far more abandoned. Worship is what we give our hearts away to in return for a promise of Life. Some worship fashion; others worship a boyfriend or husband. We really are limitless in what we will give our hearts away to. Movies, food, shopping, gossip, you name it, I've bowed before them all.

But Jesus is the only one worthy of our heart's devotion. Mary recognized who Jesus was—the source of all Life. Love Incarnate. She did what you and I hope we, too, would have done. She dropped everything and sat at his feet, fixing the gaze of her eyes and the gaze of her heart upon him.

Martha here is much like the busy church, a distracted bride. The other day I was having lunch with an old friend. Telling me about the church she was involved in, she said it was focused on the Great Commission and obeying the first commandment: to love our neighbors as ourselves. I was struck dumb. That is not the First Commandment. Jesus says the first and greatest commandment is "Love the Lord your God with all your heart and with all your soul and with all your mind" (Matt. 22:37). Jesus wants us to love one another, yes. He wants us to serve one another, yes. But first and foremost, he wants our utter devotion and love for him. It is from hearts filled with love for him that all good works and acts of love flow.

Now for one of the most beautiful mysteries of the feminine heart: women minister something to the heart of God that men do not.

Look at the record. There was an event that took place in the life of Jesus that he said should be told whenever the gospel is proclaimed around the world. It was when Mary of Bethany came and anointed him with the perfume, which cost a year's wages. It was an extravagant act of sacrificial worship, and the aroma of it filled the room. Jesus was profoundly moved by it. The men gathered there were indignant. It was a woman who did this for Christ. Just as it was also a woman who rushed into the Pharisee's house uninvited and washed Jesus' feet with her tears, dried them with her hair, and kissed them in an act of intimate, repentant worship.

It was women who followed Jesus from Galilee to care for his needs. It was women who stayed at the foot of the cross, offering him the comfort of their presence until Jesus breathed his last (only John remained with them). It was to women that Jesus first revealed himself after he rose from the dead, and it was women who first "clasped his feet and worshiped him" (Matt. 28:9) as the Risen, Victorious Lord.

Women hold a special place in the heart of God. A woman's

worship brings Jesus immense pleasure and a deep ministry. You can minister to the heart of God. You impact him. You matter. Jesus desires you to pour out your love on him in extravagant worship that ministers to his heart. This is not just for women who have the time, women who are really spiritual. You are made for romance, and the only one who can offer it to you consistently and deeply is Jesus.

Offer your heart to him.

CULTIVATING INTIMACY

When I first began to worship Jesus in the privacy of my bedroom, there was one song that I played over and over. It's a simple song made up primarily of the words:

Help us, our God.
We come to you desperately needy.

Yes. That describes *me*. I was then (and remain still) desperately needy for God. My struggle with an addiction to food and a deep loneliness were very real. I needed God to be more tangible, more real in my life. Filled with a deep hunger for his touch within my heart, thirsty for more revelation of who he truly is, and desperate for deeper healing, I began to set aside several hours each week to devote to private worship. I asked him to come.

I made room for it in my life's schedule and fought to protect the time. Whether it required unplugging the phone, arranging childcare for my young boys, or staying up after everyone was asleep, it was worth it. I became captivated by his beauty. It was rich. It was good. And it was *opposed*. To pursue intimacy with Christ, you will have to fight for it. You'll need to fight busyness (Martha's addiction). You'll need to fight accusations. You'll need to fight the Thief that would steal your Lover's gifts to you outright.

That's okay. There is a fierceness in women that was given to us for a purpose. Getting time with your Lover is worth whatever it costs.

Ask his help in making you desperately hungry for him.

Ask his help in creating the time and space you need to draw close to him.

Ask him to come, to reveal himself to you as the Lover that he is.

Go get some worship music that moves you. Not music you'd do aerobics to, but music that speaks of an intimacy with Christ. Music that draws you into intimacy with him. (One friend just told us that her current favorite is "All I Ask of You" from *Phantom of the Opera*!) Get in a private place. Let everyone know it is not a time to interrupt you. Unplug your phone. Bring your Bible and a journal to write down what you hear God say in the depths of your heart. Kneel, sit, or lie down and ask the Holy Spirit to come and help you worship Jesus. Start by telling Jesus how wonderful he is. Remember when he took care of that hard situation? Or that time he answered your prayers for financial help? Recall the times he spoke to you in your loneliness or need. Thank him for being so faithful. Stay. Linger. Worship. Let the music help usher your heart into God. Singing along with songs that proclaim "You are the One I love. You are my heart's desire. You are worthy of all praise" helps our spirit come into alignment with the truth of these words whether we feel them to be true or not.

The first time may not be amazing. You may feel your words and cries are bouncing off the ceiling. We grow in this as we practice. We practice the presence of God, as the old French monk Brother Lawrence knew. We come to God in worship not to *get* from him but to *give* to him. Jesus loves it when we offer our hearts to him in devotion. You are entering the chamber only you can enter. You are bringing something to the heart of Jesus only you can bring. You are his Betrothed, his Beloved, the beat of his heart, and the love of his life. Draw near. He is waiting.

I have always been your Lover.
Here I am.
Here I am.
—EMMYLOU HARRIS, "HERE I AM"

The culture of women in the church today is crippled by some very pervasive lies. "To be spiritual is to be busy. To be spiritual is to be disciplined. To be spiritual is to be dutiful." No, to be spiritual is to be in a Romance with God. The desire to be romanced lies deep in the heart of every woman. It is for such that you were made. And you *are* romanced, and ever will be.

CHAPTER EIGHT

Beauty to Unveil

Beauty is dangerous.
— GERARD MANLEY HOPKINS

Beauty will save the world.
—FYODOR DOSTOYEVSKY

Show me your face, let me hear your voice;
for your voice is sweet and your face is lovely.
—SONG OF SONGS 2:14

$\mathcal{T}$he essence of a man is Strength. A man is meant to be the incarnation—our experience in human form—of our Warrior God. A God *who comes through for us.*

> Who is this coming from Edom,
> from Bozrah, with his garments stained crimson?
> Who is this, robed in splendor,
> striding forward in the greatness of his strength?
> "It is I, speaking in righteousness,
> mighty to save." (Isa. 63:1)

Isn't this what makes our hearts beat more quickly, our knees weak when we watch Daniel Day-Lewis in *The Last of the Mohicans*, William Wallace in *Braveheart*, Aragorn in *The Lord of the Rings*, or Harrison Ford in nearly any of his movies? Isn't that what we, as women, long to experience from *our* man, and from the men in our lives?

To experience the strength of a man is to have him speak on our behalf. For when men abuse with words, we are pierced. Their strength has wounded us. When they are silent, we are starved. They have offered no strength; they have abandoned us. But when they speak with us, hear us, offer their words to us and on our behalf, something in our hearts is able to rest. "How are you?" is one of the simplest and most loving questions John ever asks me.

We long for the protection masculine strength offers. To have them shield us from physical harm, yes. But also to have them shield us from emotional harm and spiritual attack. To intercede for us in a relationship that has become hurtful. A friend was being verbally abused and manipulated by her mother over the phone, repeatedly. Finally, one night her husband took the phone and spoke to her mother. "You cannot talk to my wife this way. I will not allow it. You may not call again until you are ready to be kind." He did for her what she was, at that time, unable to do for herself. And she was so grateful.

As women we sometimes long for someone strong to stand between us and the vicious assaults of our Enemy. One weary night I had gone to bed early, overcome with a sense of despair and hopelessness. I felt pounded down, beyond saving, and worthy of condemnation. I lay still, engulfed in grief. Suddenly, John was at my bedside. He was angry, but not at me. John recognized the hand of our Enemy. He began to take his authority over me as my husband and forcefully commanded the minions of Satan to release me; he commanded them to be silent, and he sent them to the throne of

Jesus for judgment. When he began to pray for me, I was embarrassed. When he continued, I began to feel lighter. When he finished, tears were streaming down my face and my hands were raised to God in holy gratitude and joyful worship. I had gone to bed filled with unrelenting sorrow. I ended the night belting out heartfelt songs of praise.

Strength is what the world longs to experience from a man.

Now—isn't it obvious that we don't mean big muscles?

Of course. A man might like to work out at the gym, but if he is only physically strong, he is a hollow man. Are we satisfied as a woman with that kind of man? On the other hand, our man might prefer to read or play an instrument. Does that in any way diminish the strength of his soul? Not at all. The strength of a man is first a *soulish* strength—a strength of heart. And yes, as he lives it out, owns it, *inhabits* his strength, he does become more handsome. More attractive. As the fruit of an inner reality.

So then you can see that when we speak about the essence of a woman—her beauty—we don't mean "the perfect figure." The beauty of a woman is first a *soulish* beauty. We know—it's a harder jump to make. We've lived so long under the pressure to be beautiful. But stay with the thought for a moment, because it will really help. The beauty of a woman is first a soulful beauty. And yes, as we live it out, own it, *inhabit* our beauty, we do become more lovely. More alluring. As the poet Gerard Manley Hopkins wrote, "Self flashes off frame and face." Our true self becomes reflected in our appearance. But it flows from the inside out.

THE ESSENCE OF A WOMAN

The essence of a woman is Beauty. She is meant to be the incarnation—our experience in human form—of a Captivating God. A God *who invites us.*

Come, all you who are thirsty, come to the waters . . .
Listen, listen to me, and eat what is good,
and your soul will delight in the richest of fare. (Isa. 55:1–2)

You have stolen my heart, my sister, my bride;
you have stolen my heart
with one glance of your eyes,
with one jewel of your necklace . . .
You are a garden fountain,
a well of flowing water
streaming down from Lebanon. (Song 4:9, 15)

Beauty is what the world longs to experience from a woman. We know that. Somewhere down deep, we know it to be true. Most of our shame comes from this knowing and feeling that we have failed here. So listen to this: beauty is an essence that dwells in *every* woman. It was given to her by God. It was given to you.

Surely you would agree that God is nothing if not beautiful.

All around us God's creation shouts of his beauty and his goodness. The silhouette of lace on a barren tree draped with ice, the rays of sun streaming forth from a billowing cloud, the sound of a brook trickling over smooth stones, the form of a woman's body, and the face of a child anticipating the arrival of the ice-cream truck all speak of God's good heart if we will have but the eyes to see. The coming of spring after a hard winter is almost too glorious for a soul to bear. God's beauty is lavished on the world.

As we tried to illumine in chapter 2, Beauty is powerful. (You might want to read that passage again.) Beauty may be the most powerful thing on earth. Beauty *speaks*. Beauty *invites*. Beauty *nourishes*. Beauty *comforts*. Beauty *inspires*. Beauty is *transcendent*. Beauty draws us to God. As Simone Weil wrote, "The beauty of the world is almost the only way by which we can allow God to

penetrate us . . . Beauty captivates the senses in order to obtain permission to pass straight through to the soul . . . The soul's inclination to love beauty is the trap God most frequently uses in order to win it."

God has given this Beauty to Eve, to every woman. Beauty is core to a woman—who she is and what she longs to be—and one of the most glorious ways we bear the image of God in a broken and often ugly world. It's messy to talk about. It's mysterious. And that should not surprise us. Women are creatures of great mystery; not problems to be solved but mysteries to be enjoyed. And that, too, is part of her glory.

Women want to impact their world for good. As corulers with Adam, we are created to do so, and one of the key ways we influence our world is in making it a more beautiful place to live. We decorate our homes. We put flowers on the table. Pioneer women brought china teacups into the wilderness, and I bring a pretty tablecloth to eat on when my family camps. We wear perfume, paint our toenails, color our hair, and pierce our ears, all in an effort to be ever more beautiful.

Beauty is the most *essential* and, yes, the most *misunderstood* of all the feminine qualities. We want you to hear clearly that it is an essence every woman carries from the moment of her creation. The only things standing in the way of our beauty are our doubts and fears, and the hiding and striving we fall to as a result.

BEAUTY FLOWS FROM A HEART AT REST

Janet is twenty-one. She was on the dance team in high school. Small and petite with a fabulous figure. Unlike so many women in that world of competitive beauty, she escaped an eating disorder. But she runs between five and ten miles *a day*. She watches what she eats. She's able to wear the cutest clothes. And yet . . . when you're

with her, your heart does not rest. Her beauty impresses, but it does not invite. The reason is simple: she is striving. She is a perfectionist (an extra two pounds is a crisis; a pimple is a disaster). Her beauty feels tenuous, shaky. It is not flowing from her heart. It's almost as if it's forced, from the outside, through discipline and fear.

June is one of the most beautiful women we have ever met. We encountered her a few years ago while doing a retreat on the coast of North Carolina. Her hair was long, swept up loosely and held by decorative combs. She wore unique, dangly earrings and pretty flowing skirts. Her eyes sparkled when she laughed, which she did often, and her smile lit up the room. She was clearly in love with her husband, her face adoring as she gazed at him. June was at rest with herself, at home in who she was. Talking with her, just being with her, made us feel more at rest with ourselves as well. Her spacious, beautiful soul invited others to come, to be, to taste and see that the Lord is good, whatever was happening in your life. She wept at the retreat. She laughed at the retreat. She was gloriously alive and in love, both with her husband and with the God of the Universe.

And June was about seventy-five years old.

What is the difference between these two women? Rest. June's beauty flows from a heart at rest.

You see, beauty indwells *every* woman. We've seen it so many times counseling women of all ages. Like a shy doe, it reveals itself for a moment, then fades back into cover. Usually it comes when she doesn't know it, when she isn't trying to make it come. Rather, something is happening that allows her defenses to come down for a moment. For instance, when someone is listening. She knows that she matters. Someone cares about her heart, wants to know her. Her beauty emerges as if from behind a veil.

So the choice a woman makes is not to conjure beauty but to let her defenses down. To choose to set aside her normal means of survival and just let her heart show up. Beauty comes with it.

> Your beauty should not come from outward adornment, such as braided hair and the wearing of gold jewelry and fine clothes. Instead, it should be that of your inner self, the unfading beauty of a gentle and quiet spirit. (1 Peter 3:3–4)

First, Peter is not saying that we shouldn't enjoy wearing pretty things. What he's trying to say is that true beauty *comes from* the inner part of us. Our hearts. A heart at rest. When I first read the part about a gentle and quiet spirit, I gave up having much hope of ever making the grade. I am loud. I make jokes when I am nervous or uncomfortable, and when I am comfortable and at ease. I am not prone to long silences. If no one is talking in a group, I take that as an invitation to share my thoughts. A gentle and quiet spirit? Oh dear.

I began to include in my prayers for sanctification a complete personality transplant. Yes, put an angel at the edge of my tongue to guard my every word. And while you're at it, make me someone else, please. Someone more like Melanie in *Gone with the Wind*. Or Mother Teresa. Someone really *good*. I believed this was not too much to ask. He is the God of miracles, after all.

God, in his faithfulness, is changing me. But I remain an extrovert. In fact, instead of making me into someone else, he is making me more *me*. And that is one of the beautiful things about him. That the more *his* we become, the more ourselves we become; more our true selves. So it is a good thing that I misunderstood the Scripture. Peter doesn't mean that beautiful women rarely speak above a whisper, if they speak at all. No. To have a gentle and quiet spirit is to have a heart of faith, a heart that trusts in God, a spirit that has been quieted by his love and filled with his peace. Not a heart that is striving and restless.

A woman in her glory, a woman of beauty, is a woman who is not striving to become beautiful or worthy or enough. She knows

136

in her quiet center where God dwells that he finds her beautiful, has deemed her worthy, and in him, she is enough. *In fact, the only thing getting in the way of our being fully captivating and enjoyed is our striving.*

"He will quiet you with his love" (Zeph. 3:17). A woman of true beauty is a woman who in the depths of her soul is at rest, trusting God because she has come to know him to be worthy of her trust. She exudes a sense of calm, a sense of rest, and invites those around her to rest as well. She speaks comfort; she knows that we live in a world at war, that we have a vicious enemy, and our journey is through a broken world. But she also knows that because of God all is well, that all will be well. *A woman of true beauty offers others the grace to be and the room to become.* In her presence, we can release the tension and pressure that so often grip our hearts. We can also breathe in the truth that God loves us and he is good.

This is why we must keep asking. Ask Jesus to show you your beauty. Ask him what he thinks of you *as a woman.* His words to us let us rest and unveil our beauty.

BEAUTY IS INVITING

Many years ago our family was staying with friends at their little cabin in an old mountain town in Colorado. One morning as we drove to a remote area where we planned to take a hike, we passed a home that was surrounded by a garden of stunning beauty. I haven't seen anything like it before or since. Groves of towering delphiniums, profuse foxgloves, oases of dianthus and pansies, clematis and roses caught my eyes and my heart. Later that day I returned. I needed to get closer to that garden. I needed to get into it. I wanted to immerse myself in its extravagance. Emboldened by my desire, I walked up to the front door and knocked.

A small, elderly woman answered the door and eyed me with

suspicion. I quickly introduced myself as a visitor who had seen her garden, been completely captured by it, and wondered if I could, *please*, walk around in it. Her wariness melted into delight. Enjoy my garden? Enjoy the creative work of my hands? Enjoy the fruit of my labor? You betcha. She came out to show me the garden herself, and we spent a wonderful afternoon together. The next morning I was back, having been invited to bring the whole family.

Beauty beckons us. Beauty invites us. *Come, explore, immerse yourself.* God—Beauty himself—invites us to know him. "Taste and see that the LORD is good" (Ps. 34:8). He delights in alluring us and in revealing himself to those who wholeheartedly seek him. He wants to be known, to be explored. A woman does too. She fears it, but below the fear is a longing to be known, to be seen as beautiful and enjoyed. So the unveiled beauty of a woman entices and invites. The heart of the woman determines *what* it is she is inviting others *to*—to life or to death.

Proverbs speaks about two different women, two archetypes. One is Lady Folly; the other, Lady Wisdom. Both are lovely. Both set their tables with fine food and aged wine and dress in fine linens. Both call to the passersby to come in, taste, eat, linger. Lady Folly's door is the mouth of an open grave. Lady Wisdom's home is the passageway to discernment, holiness, and Life.

A woman who is striving invites others to strive. The message—sometimes implicit in her actions, sometimes explicit through her words—is, "Get your act together. Life is uncertain. There is no time for your heart here. Shape up. Get busy. That's what is important." She does not say, "All is well. All shall be well." Her fear doesn't allow it. She is withholding the very things her world needs.

By contrast a woman whose heart is at rest invites others to rest. That's what we felt in June's presence—and in the presence of many women we know and have come to love. We are invited to be ourselves. Remember the traffic analogy we used in chapter 2—the exhaust, the noises, the tension? Compare that to what it's like to come into a beautiful place—a garden or meadow or quiet beach. You find room for your soul. It expands. You can breathe again. You can rest. It is good. That is what it is like to be with a beautiful woman. You are free to be you. It is one of life's greatest gifts.

A woman who is hiding invites others to do the same. "Don't be vulnerable. Hide yourself." A woman who makes herself vulnerable and available for intimacy invites others to do the same. After all, Eve is the incarnation of the heart of God for intimacy. She says to the world, through her invitation to relationship, "You are wanted here. We want to know you. Come in. Share yourself. Be enjoyed. Enjoy me as I share myself." A woman who is controlling cannot invite others to rest, to be known. They will feel controlled in her presence. It won't feel safe there.

A woman who is unveiling her beauty is inviting others to life. She risks being vulnerable; exposing her true heart and inviting others to share theirs. She is not demanding, but she is hopeful. When our assistant Cherie walks into the room, it feels as if someone has just opened up the windows and let the fresh air in. Cherie is young, but that does not stop her from offering her kindness, her hopefulness, her sincere interest in how you are. She offers her beauty by asking good questions and by bringing something of her times with God—an insight, a glimpse into his heart—to bear. She entices others to the heart of God.

You see, ultimately, a woman invites us to know God. To experience through her that God is merciful. That he is tender and kind. That God longs for us—to be known by us and to know us. She invites us to experience that God is good, deep, lovely, alluring. Captivating.

We know many of you are feeling, *But I'm not there. I'm not that kind of woman.* Here is where we "work out" our salvation as God works in us (Phil. 2:12–13). As you begin to live like this, you discover the places in your heart that still need the healing touch of Jesus. That's how it goes. We don't get to stay in hiding until we are whole; Jesus invites us to live as an inviting woman now, and find our healing along the way.

OFFERING BEAUTY

Beauty overwhelms us, enchants us, fascinates us, and calls us.
—FR. ANDREW GREELEY

For a woman to unveil her beauty means she is offering her heart. Not primarily her works or her usefulness (think Martha in the kitchen). Offering her *presence.* At family gatherings my (Stasi here) mother hid in the kitchen. She cooked and baked and prepared and served and cleaned, and for the life of us, we couldn't get her out of there. We wanted her to share her life with us, her thoughts and her ideas, not just her efforts. She wouldn't come. And we were less because of it.

The gift of presence is a rare and beautiful gift. To come—unguarded, undistracted—and be fully present, fully engaged with whoever we are with at that moment. Have you noticed in reading the Gospels that people enjoyed being around Jesus? They wanted to be near him—to share a meal, take a walk, have a lingering conversation. It was the gift of his presence. When you were with him, you felt he was offering you his heart. When we offer our unguarded presence, we live like Jesus. And we invite others to do the same.

Whenever we are with our friend Jan, there is always an offer and an invitation. She really wants to know how we are, what battles we've been facing, what God is doing in our lives. And she truly offers herself. Sometimes it's her laughter and a wry joke. Sometimes it's her tears from an old sorrow. She offers herself, her beauty, to us. She invites us to live above the striving of the world. She gives something of God.

Beauty offers mercy. My son Samuel is entering adolescence. My little boy is becoming a man. Sometimes it's hard for me to let go. Sometimes his sullen attitude makes me mad. Boys-becoming-men are hard for a woman to understand. They act as if they don't need us anymore. Sometimes they act rudely in their emerging strength. I want to "come down" on him. (It always backfires when I do.) But that is not what he needs from me. He needs mercy. A kind word, a smile. Grace at the end of the day. He softens toward me, and our relationship is recovered. A woman who is full of tender mercy and soft vulnerability is a powerful, lovely woman.

Beauty isn't demanding. Instead, it speaks from *desire*. When our children were young, John had to travel *a lot* for work. On his days off, he was pursuing a master's degree in counseling. That did not leave much time for our family. It fell to me to pay the bills, run the home, and parent the boys. Two of them were in Little League baseball; our youngest was still in diapers. I was busy. I was tired. I couldn't do it. I still remember the fear I felt when I asked John to sit down and talk. I told him that I couldn't do this family thing without him. I told him that I needed him. I asked for his help. I didn't demand him to come through. I didn't whine. I expressed my need and invited his strength, his presence. To my surprise, John told me that in my vulnerability to him, I had never been more feminine or more beautiful.

To offer your heart is to offer your desire—instead of your demand. Beauty offers desire. Our friend Tammy was in a bad marriage. Her husband was verbally abusive. Rather than becoming hard and cynical, she remained soft. Rather than just giving up, she held on to her desire for something more with him. Instead of demanding, she simply would put her desire before him. "Don't you want more for us?" It was beautiful. Even though he chose not to respond, she retained her feminine beauty and offered it as much as she could.

OF COURSE IT FEELS RISKY

The scariest thing for a man is to offer his strength in situations where he doesn't know if it will make any difference. Or worse, that he will fail. Remember, a man's deepest Question is, *Do I have what it takes?* Failure says, *No.* And that is why most men avoid any situation where they might fail. They fear exposure. They fear it will be discovered that they are not a man.

Given the fact that we live after the Fall, far from Eden, and that a man's life is plagued by "thorns and thistles," *most* situations feel like a test of his strength. There is simply no guarantee of success. That's why some men won't play sports. They fear exposure, fear being seen as weak. That's why other men would rather work late than come home and talk to their wives or their children. They know what to do at work; they don't know what to do in their most important relationships. A man's basic sin is his choice to offer strength only in those situations where he knows things will go well. And so repentance for a man is entering into the very situations that he fears and offering his strength anyway.

If he fears intimacy, then offering strength means offering intimacy. If he fears failing in his career, offering his strength means taking a promotion or accepting a new and risky project. If he fears standing up for his children against an angry school principal, then standing up for them is what he must do. If he fears committing to the woman he's been dating for five years, then offering strength is buying her a ring. If he fears initiating sex with his wife, then offering strength means initiating sexual intimacy.

In the same way, the scariest thing for women is to offer our beauty into situations where we don't know if it will make any difference. Or worse, that we will be rejected. For our Question is, *Am I lovely?* And to be rejected is to hear a resounding, *No.* A woman doesn't want to offer her beauty unless she is guaranteed that it will be well received. But life offers no such guarantees. We, too, must take risks.

A few verses after Peter talks about a quiet heart, he gives us what might be the secret to releasing a woman's heart and her beauty:

Do not give way to fear. (1 Peter 3:6)

Isn't that why we hide, why we strive, why we control, why we do anything *but* offer beauty? We are afraid. We have given way to fear. Just think about your life—why you do the things you do. Have you asked yourself how much you are motivated by fear? Janet's beauty regimen is totally motivated by fear. She doesn't believe she's beautiful. She believes she's ugly. So she strives. June would not let fear in.

That is why God says to us, "In repentance and rest is your salvation, in quietness and trust is your strength" (Isa. 30:15). In repentance and rest. He loves it when we, gripped with doubt and fear that he will not be enough, turn the gaze of our souls to him in hope. He loves to prove himself faithful and more than enough to satisfy our hungry souls. When we do turn to him, our souls rest and we are saved. Again. And again.

We can't wait until we feel safe to love and invite. In fact, if you feel a little scared, then you're probably on the right path. Of course it's scary. It's vulnerable. It's naked. God calls us to stop hiding, to stop dominating, to trust him, and to offer our true selves. He wants us to bring to bear the weight of our lives and all that he has given to us, worked into us, and offer it to our world. To entice, allure, and invite others to Jesus by reflecting his glory in our lives. He will give no guarantee that others will enjoy us and respond well.

In fact, we can be sure that there will be times when they do not. Jesus offered like no other, and many rejected him. In those moments or seasons when that happens to us, God's invitation is to bring our sorrow to him. Not to shut down with, *I'll never try that again.* But to keep our hearts open and alive, and find refuge and healing in his love.

Our friend Melissa is married to a man who is not present, who doesn't "get her." Yet. She has known many lonely years. But Melissa has discovered romance with God, and her heart rests in him. She offers her beauty in so many ways. She works as a teacher of women's Bible studies and Christian literature. When you hear her present her ideas, they don't come across as precepts to believe but invitations to see. She allures others to the heart of God. She invites her husband to come closer. Beauty invites. How he responds—if he responds—is not in her hands. But still, she invites.

Linda is in constant pain. Arthritis in her bones runs throughout her body, from her legs to the back of her neck. Her husband divorced her a few years ago, but Linda's heart has been romanced, awakened by the Lover of her soul. She has chosen to remain alive and present. She offers her beauty in her counseling practice, walking alongside clients into deeper realms of brokenness and ultimately healing. She offers such beauty to her children. And to her friends. She invites others to the heart of God. These women remind us that it can be done—we, too, can risk offering our hearts of beauty despite enormous risk. They happen to be two of the most beautiful women we know. And their beauty has *deepened* as they've chosen this path.

LETTING OUR HEARTS BE DEEPENED

As we increasingly become women of substance, women who offer true beauty, we find that our hearts grow in their capacity to love and be loved, to desire, to live. Our hearts are enlarged by Jesus.

And by that, we mean that we must be willing to be honest with him and with ourselves about the true nature of our souls—our sorrows, our desires, our dreams, our fears, our deepest and scariest hopes. To invite Jesus to come and walk with us there, to remove from our hearts the things that are getting in the way of our loving. We do not always get what we want, but that doesn't mean that we no longer want. It means we stay awake to the unmet longing and ache. Wait there. Invite Jesus to come, there.

And he will come. Not always to satisfy us by giving us what we want. But to come himself; to meet us with his very Person and to satisfy us with himself.

To possess true beauty, we must be willing to suffer. I don't like that. Just writing it down makes my heart shrink back. Yet, if Christ himself was perfected through his sufferings, why would I believe God would not do the same with me? Women who are stunningly beautiful are women who have had their hearts enlarged by suffering. By saying yes when the world says no. By paying the high price of loving truly and honestly without demanding that they be loved in return. And by refusing to numb their pain in the myriad of ways available. They have come to know that when everyone and everything has left them, God is there. They have learned, along with David, that those who go through the desolate valley will find it a place of springs (Ps. 84:6).

Living in true beauty can require much waiting, much time, much tenacity of spirit. We must constantly direct our gazes toward the face of God, even in the presence of longing and sorrow. It is in the waiting that our hearts are enlarged. The waiting does not diminish us. As a pregnant woman is enlarged in her waiting, so are our hearts. God does not always rescue us out of a painful season. You know that he does not always give to us what we so desperately want when we want it. He is after something much more valuable than our happiness. Much more substantive than our health. He is restoring and growing in us an eternal weight of glory. And some-times . . . it hurts.

But the experience of sorrow in no way diminishes the joy of living. Rather, it enhances it. When my (Stasi's) mother was in the last few days of her life, we sat together on a bench in Dana Point, California, overlooking the Pacific Ocean. Watching the powerful blue waves crash over the rocks, feeling the warmth of the sun on our faces, we turned to watch white doves soaring on the wind. We were silenced by the beauty of it all, by sharing in the beauty together, and by knowing that it was the last time we would share it on this side of life.

Knowing the parting that was soon to come did not diminish the beauty nor our delight in being together. No, it heightened it. It made us more alive to the moment. More aware. More present. And so it is with a heart awakened to its sorrow. It is more aware, more present, and more alive, to all of the facets of life.

CULTIVATING BEAUTY

Every woman possesses a captivating beauty. Every woman. But for most of us it has been long buried, wounded, and captive. It takes time for it to emerge into wholeness. It needs to be cultivated, restored, set free.

How do we cultivate beauty? How do we become ever more beautiful? By tending to our hearts with great care, as a master gardener tends to her work.

> My mother's sons were angry with me
> and made me take care of the vineyards;
> my own vineyard I have neglected. (Song 1:6)

Yes, life is harsh on a woman's heart. It has been hard on your heart. The assault on our beauty is real. But Jesus is urging us now to care for ourselves, watch over our hearts (Prov. 4:23). The world needs your beauty. That is why you are here. Your heart and your beauty are something to be treasured and nourished. And it takes time. Every gardener knows this. In our age of instant makeovers and microwave meals, we don't like to wait. But a newly planted rose's presentation in its first year is nothing compared to its second. If properly cared for, its second year's display doesn't hold a candle to its third. Gardens need to become established; their roots need to go deep through summer rains and winter frosts. A garden's beauty does not diminish with age; rather it takes years for it to become all that it can become.

Our hearts need to feed on beauty to sustain them. We need times of solitude and silence. We need times of refreshment and laughter and rest. We need to listen to the voice of God in our hearts as he tells us what we need. Sometimes it will be a bubble bath. Sometimes it is going for a run or a movie or taking a nap. Often, Jesus will call us away to spend precious time alone with him. We grow in our intimacy with Jesus as we practice listening to his urging, his nudges within. Pay attention to them and follow. The Holy Spirit is our guide, our counselor, our comforter, our Great Friend, and he will lead us. Abiding in Christ means paying attention to the voice of God within, nourishing our own hearts and nourishing our relationship with him. Over time.

Contrary to what the world claims, Beauty does not diminish with time; Beauty deepens and increases. As with June, gorgeous at seventy-five, we find that our latter glory will be greater than our former (Hag. 2:9). True beauty comes from a depth of soul that can only be attained through living many years well. June was seventy-five and captivating.

I will never forget her because she gave me such hope. I finally understood that it took *that long* to become *that beautiful.* Beauty such as hers is rare because it is a rare woman who chooses to keep her heart alive in this dangerous world. Without striving. Her heart was very much alive. Present. Open. Alluring. She had lived years in the presence of God, with the gaze of her heart fixed on him. As we gaze on Jesus, as we behold his goodness, his glory, we are changed into his likeness, the most beautiful Person of all.

> They looked to Him and were radiant. (Ps. 34:5 NKJV)

We have all heard it said that a woman is most beautiful when she is in love. It's true. You've seen it yourself. When a woman knows that she is loved and loved deeply, she glows from the inside. This radiance stems from a heart that has had its deepest questions answered. *Am I lovely? Am I worth fighting for? Have I been and will I continue to be romanced?* When these questions are answered yes, a restful, quiet spirit settles in a woman's heart.

And every woman can have these questions answered yes. You have been and you will continue to be romanced all your life. Yes. Our God finds you lovely. Jesus has moved heaven and earth to win you for himself. He will not rest until you are completely his. The King is enthralled by your beauty. He finds you captivating.

Beauty is a quality of the soul that expresses itself in the visible world. You can see it. You can touch it. You are drawn to it. Beauty illuminates. Its essence, says Thomas Aquinas, is its "luminosity." It is bound up with the immortal. Beauty flows from a heart that is alive. We have known women you might describe as "frumpy," who seemed to care nothing for their appearance. We have seen them become women who possessed great beauty. We watched it grow in them as they discovered that they were deeply loved, as their hearts came alive in response to the Great Romancer. We *are* romanced. We *are* loved. When we are at rest in that knowledge, we can offer our hearts to others and invite them to Life.

FAITH, HOPE, AND LOVE

Unveiling our beauty really just means unveiling our feminine hearts.

It's scary, for sure. That is why it is our greatest expression of faith, because we are going to have to trust Jesus—really trust him. We'll have to trust him that we *have* a beauty, that what he has said of us is true. And we'll have to trust him with how it goes when we offer it, because that is out of our control. We'll have to trust him when it hurts, and we'll have to trust him when we are finally seen and enjoyed. That's why unveiling our beauty is *how* we live by faith.

Unveiling our beauty is our greatest expression of hope. We hope that it will matter, that our beauty really does make a difference. We hope there is a greater and higher Beauty, hope we are reflecting that Beauty, and hope it will triumph. Our hope is that all is well because of Jesus and that all will be well because of him. So we unveil beauty in hope. And finally, we unveil beauty in the hope that Jesus is *growing* our beauty. Yes, we are not yet what we long to be. But we are underway. Restoration has begun. To offer beauty now is an expression of hope that it will be completed.

And unveiling beauty is our greatest expression of love, because it is what the world most needs from us. When we choose not to hide, when we choose to offer our hearts, we are choosing to love. Jesus offers; he invites; he is present. That is how he loves. That is how we love—sincerely, as the Scripture says, "from the heart" (1 Peter 1:22). Our focus shifts from self-protection to the hearts of others. We offer Beauty so that their hearts might come alive, be healed, know God. That is love.

CHAPTER NINE

Arousing Adam

❦

Are you strong enough to be my man?
—SHERYL CROW

Come away, my lover,
and be like a gazelle
or like a young stag
on the spice-laden mountains.
—SONG OF SONGS 8:14

*W*hen it comes to the subject of loving a man—any of the men in your life—we need far more than a chapter. A book would barely feel sufficient. The issues are often murky, and things can get really muddy as time goes by. But we cannot pass over this either. It's far too important; too many questions linger here for most women. So we will try and lay out in this chapter the deeper issues, and trust the Holy Spirit to help you with the application. (Too many books offer techniques and tips and rules without explaining the issues of the *heart* that lie behind them.) You are a woman, after all, not a child. Your heart can figure this out.

Everything we said about unveiling beauty, about how a woman invites and offers—this is *so* much more true when it comes to loving Adam. (We'll bet you were thinking about the man in your life through most of the last chapter.) True femininity arouses true masculinity. Think about it—all those heroes in all those tales play the hero *because* there is a woman in his life, a true Beauty who is his inspiration. It's that simple and that profound. True femininity calls forth true masculinity. We awaken it, arouse it in a way that nothing else on earth even comes close to.

Adam's Wound

If you watch little boys for any length of time, you'll see how deeply the Hero is written on their hearts. I just saw a mom with a little guy at the grocery store. He must have been all of three. He was dressed in his jammies that had this really cool super hero cape sewn into the shoulders. I'll wager she doesn't normally let him go out midday still in his jammies. I'll bet what happened was she couldn't get him to take them off. Boys love to dress up as army men, Jedi knights, cowboys, heroes. Their games are filled with battle and courage and testing. Who's brave enough to jump out the second story window onto the trampoline?

When they become teenagers, young boys take on an air of independence and bravado that can really drive moms nuts. It looks arrogant and defiant, but it is their masculine strength emerging in an awkward stage. They race cars and care about what they wear and strut their stuff. As Bruce Springsteen sang, "The girls comb their hair in rearview mirrors and the boys try to look so hard." In all of this, you can see their Question: *Do I have what it takes? Am I the real deal? Am I a man?*

A man's deepest wounds come from the way his Question was answered in his youth. Just like yours. Every man is wounded. As he was growing up, he looked to his father to answer his Question. The result was often devastating.

In the case of violent fathers, the wound is given directly. Dave tried to intervene in an argument between his mom and dad when he was about thirteen. Like a good man should, he stepped in to protect his mom. His father leveled his resentment right at his son's heart: "You are such a mama's boy." He's fought that sentence now for more than a decade. He wants so badly to pursue a woman, but something in him feels young and "not man enough." After all, he was told he wasn't a man; he was a mama's boy. Charles's father was a jock, but Charles was a pianist. One day his father just lost it. Who knows what else had built up in his soul or between them, but he came home to find Charles at the piano, and he said with contempt, "You're a faggot." Charles never played the piano again. And he is finding it hard to commit to the woman in his life. Something in him feels . . . uncertain. Unmanly.

Passive fathers also wound, often leaving the boy's Question *un*answered. His silence leaves a vacuum for fear and doubt to fill. That's where my drivenness came from. My dad was wrestling with some pretty awful battles of his own, especially when I was a teenager, and in many ways he left me to face mine alone. I felt . . . abandoned by him. He left me without an answer to my deepest Question. For the next twenty years I was a frightened, driven perfectionist, running hard to keep from facing my wounds. I was afraid that in fact I was just a boy in a man's world, and I kept overachieving to prove I was a man.

Adam's sin and Adam's woundedness come together to result in the passivity or the drivenness you find in so many men. Why won't he talk to me? Why won't he commit? Why is he so angry? Why is he violent? You won't begin to understand a man until you understand his Question, his wound, and how Adam also fell. His search for validation is the driving force of his life.

Just like yours.

Standing in Love's Way

In *Wild at Heart* I warned men that the greatest obstacle to loving a woman was this: too many men take their Question to Eve. They look to her for the validation of their souls. (Haven't you felt it?) It happens usually around adolescence, this fatal shift. The father has been silent or violent; his chance to redeem his son is nearly gone. The next window that opens in a boy's journey is his sexuality. Suddenly, he is aware of Eve. She looks like life itself to him. She looks like the answer to his Question.

It's a fatal shift. So much of the pornography addiction for men comes from this. It's not about sex—it's about validation. She makes him feel like a man. She offers him her beauty, and it makes him feel strong. This is also the root of most affairs. Some woman comes along and offers to answer his Question. His wife has been giving him an F, and she comes along and says, "You're an A to me," and he's history. If he hasn't found that deep validation he needs from God, he's a sitting duck.

I've tried in every way to help men understand that no woman can tell you who you are as a man. Masculinity is bestowed by masculinity. It cannot come from any other source. Yes—a woman can offer a man so much. She can be his *ezer*, his companion, his inspiration. But she cannot be the validation of his soul. As men, we have *got* to take our Question to God, to our Father in heaven. Only he knows who we truly are. Only he can pronounce the verdict on us. A man goes to Eve to *offer* his strength. He does not go to her to *get* it.

Now, the same holds true for you, Eve.

You cannot take your Question to Adam. You cannot look to him for the validation of your soul. But *so* many women do. *If I have a man, then I'm okay. Then I'm loved.* It happens around adolescence for women too. The time for her father to speak into her life begins to wane. A new window opens up—boys. And if her father has not been there for her, she is starving for love, and she'll give herself to boys in the hope of finding it. Remember the old maxim "Girls give sex to get love"? It's true.

Mary Pipher's well-known book *Reviving Ophelia* documents this tragic shift in adolescent girls. This almost total loss of self. Girls who were confident and courageous in their youth become uncertain in their teens. Girls who used to have lots of interests and opinions and dreams suddenly seem depressed, lost, obsessed about their looks and about the attention of boys. The shift, at its root, is simply this: they have taken their Question to Adam. It is a deadly shift.

What makes this seem so natural, especially for women, is that Eve *was* made for Adam. "It is not good for the man to be alone. I will make [an *ezer kenegdo*] for him" (Gen. 2:18). Eve was literally fashioned from the rib taken out of Adam's side. There is an incompleteness that haunts us, makes us yearn for one another. How many of you sighed at the end of *Jerry Maguire*, when he runs through the airport and races across town to get back to his wife, who has separated from him? He says, "You complete me." That is true; it's part of the man-woman design.

And yet.

No man can tell you who you are as a woman. No man is the verdict on your soul. (Dear sister, how many of you have lost yourself in this search?) One woman said to us, "I still feel useless. I am not a woman. I do not have a man. I have failed to captivate someone." The ache is real. But the verdict is false. Only God can tell you who you are. Only God can speak the answer you need to hear. That is why we spoke of the Romance with him first. It comes first. It must. It has to. Adam is a far too unreliable source—amen!

Now, yes, in a loving relationship, we are meant to speak to one another's wounds. In love we can bring such deep joy and healing as we offer to one another our strength and beauty. It means the world for me to have Stasi say, "You are such a man."

And, it means the world to have John say to me, "Stasi, you are a beautiful woman."

We can—and should—offer this to one another. This is one way our love helps to heal our mate's wound. But our *core* validation, our *primary* validation has to come from God. And until it does, until we look to him for the healing of our souls, our relationships are really hurt by looking to each other for something only God can give.

Complicating matters further is the curse upon Eve. "Your desire will be for your husband, and he will rule over you" (Gen. 3:16). There is an ache in Eve now that she tries to get Adam to fill. There is an emptiness given to her to drive her back to God, but she takes it to Adam instead. It makes a mess of many good relationships. You know all about this. No matter how much Adam pours into your aching soul, it's never enough. He cannot fill you. Maybe he's pulled away because he senses you're asking him to fill you. Every woman has to reckon with this—this ache she tries to get her man to fill. In order to learn how to love him, you *must* first stop insisting that he fill you.

We say all this as a sort of prologue because we cannot talk about loving a man well—whoever he might be in your life—until we see that we cannot look to him for things he cannot give. We cannot love Adam while we are looking to him to validate us. It will usher in too much fear. If he's the verdict on us as a woman, we won't be able to truly and freely offer him our beauty. We'll hold it back in fear. Or we'll give ourselves over to him in inappropriate ways, in a sort of sexual or emotional promiscuity, desperate for his attention. And we won't be able to confront him and stand up to him when he needs *that* from us as well.

Ask Jesus to show you what you've been doing with your Question and how you've related to Adam. Only then can we talk about loving men.

How Does a Woman Love a Man?

Let's start with sex.

Not because "it's all men think about" (as many a cynical woman has said), but because it presents the relationship between femininity and masculinity in such a clear way. It is a beautiful and rich metaphor, a very passionate and heightened picture for a much broader reality. The question before us is, how does a woman best love a man? The answer is simple: Entice him. Inspire him. *Allure* him.

Think of a woman on her wedding night. She dims the lights and puts on a silky something that accentuates the loveliness of her body, reveals the beauty of her naked form, yet also leaves something yet to be unveiled. She puts on perfume and lipstick and checks her hair. She *allures* her man. She hopes to arouse him and invite him to come to her and enter her. In an act of stunning vulnerability she takes life's greatest risk—offering her unveiled beauty to him, opening herself up to him in every way.

And as for her man, if he does not rise to the occasion, nothing will happen. There will be no consummation of love, no life conceived unless the man is able to offer his strength to his woman. That is how we make love. Femininity is what arouses his masculinity. His strength is what makes a woman yearn to be beautiful.

It's that simple, that beautiful, that mysterious, and incredibly profound.

The beauty of a woman is what arouses the strength of a man. He *wants* to play the man when a woman acts like that. You can't hold him back. He *wants* to come through. And this desire is crucial. Don't you want him to *want* to come through for you? Not to be forced to, not because he "ought to." But because he *wants* to come through. Well then, arouse his desire. In any facet of life.

Can you imagine what it would be like if a young bride took

the approach toward her new husband that so many women take in other matters? Imagine her getting out her day planner and asking, "When would you like to have sex this week?" (The Efficient Woman.) Or commenting to her new husband, "I suppose you'll want to have sex tonight. Let's get it over with early—I have a lot to do in the morning." (The Busy Woman.) Or the more direct challenge, "That was a pretty poor performance last night. You wanna try it again?" (The Demanding Woman.)

You get the idea. Your message to your man is either, "Sugar, you have what it takes," or, "I don't think you are much of a man. Want to prove me wrong?" The same is true for a woman. Your heart responds very differently to the *pressure* to be beautiful, "You're going out in *that?*" as opposed to the *assurance* that you *are* beautiful, "Sweetheart, you look so lovely tonight." A woman wants to feel beautiful. The strength of a good man makes her feel so. A man wants to feel strong. The beauty of a good woman makes him feel so. This principle plays out far beyond sex and marriage.

KNOWING HIS STORY

Men may sometimes joke or moan that women are a mystery to them. And, well, we often are! But the opposite holds true as well. I live in a household of four men, and they are often a mystery to me. I know many, many women who experience the same kind of befuddlement. It is immensely helpful to understand the man in your life by coming to know his story. What was life like growing up for him? How was the deep question of his heart answered? Did he know he was loved? Was he encouraged as a boy and as a man? Was he told he "has what it takes"? What is he still living with and under?

Pursue your man by inviting him to tell you his story; the story of his childhood, his teen years. Ask him about good memories and bad ones. Really listen. Growing in your understanding of where your man is coming from will help you to love him, have mercy for him, and give you the ability to encourage him to pursue his own healing and live differently.

THE HOLY, SCANDALOUS WOMEN OF THE BIBLE

There are five women mentioned in the genealogy of Jesus. Now, that might not strike you as a big deal, until you understand that women are never mentioned in those genealogies. It's *always* men. "The father of so-and-so, the son of so-and-so." They read like baseball scorecards. When Matthew adds a few women to the cast, it is a major and notable exception. These woman are so important to God that he has the writer break all cultural norms and even open himself to criticism and dismissal in order to make a point: "Look here—these are *really* good women."

Of course, Mary the mother of Jesus is mentioned. There is also the Bible-study favorite, Ruth. And Rahab and Tamar. What distinguishes these women? Different situations, different acts of obedience. Yet the common theme is this: *Courage, Cunning,* and *Stunning Vulnerability.* Mary is an amazing young woman. Maybe fifteen or so. She accepts the mission God brings to her even though it will cost her dearly. Really now—a young girl known to be seeing an older man turns up pregnant, claiming she's been impregnated by God? She is virtuous, but her choice will be seen by others as scandalous all her life. She makes herself vulnerable—staggeringly vulnerable (she could be stoned for this; certainly she will be abandoned and ostracized)—in order to follow God.

Tamar's story is difficult and beautiful, one we haven't time for here. But one worth wrestling with. (You can find it in Genesis 38.) She uses cunning in the face of men who are failing her badly in order to expose their sin and invite (not demand) them to come through. Rahab is another scandalous story. She's the woman who committed treason in order to walk with God and save her family. (She hid the spies of Israel when they came to her city, Jericho, on a preinvasion reconnaissance mission—in open defiance of her government.) We haven't heard any Bible studies on that one either. "When Treason Becomes Essential for a Woman." And there is Ruth. This is how I explained her story in *Wild at Heart*:

> Ruth, as you'll remember, is the daughter-in-law of a woman from Judah named Naomi. Both women have lost their husbands and are in a pretty bad way; they have no man looking out for them, their financial status is below the poverty line, and they are vulnerable in many other ways as well. Things begin to look up when Ruth catches the eye of a wealthy single man named Boaz. Boaz is a good man, this we know. He offers her some protection and some food. But Boaz is not giving Ruth what she really needs—a ring.
>
> So what does Ruth do? She "inspires" him. She arouses him to be a man. Here's the scene: The men have been working dawn till dusk to bring in the barley harvest; they've just finished and now it's party time. Ruth takes a bubble bath and puts on a knockout dress; then she waits for the right moment. That moment happens to be late in the evening after Boaz has finished celebrating: "When Boaz had finished eating and drinking and was in good spirits, he went over to lie down at the far end of the grain pile. Ruth approached quietly, uncovered his feet and lay down" (Ruth 3:7). Note the gentle phrase, "good spirits." The King James describes it as "had a merry heart," a result of the wine at the party.
>
> There is no possible reading of this passage that is "safe" or "nice." Yes, there are folks that'll try to tell you that it's perfectly common for a beautiful single woman "in that culture" to

Captivating

approach a single man (who's had too much to drink) in the middle of the night with no one else around (the far side of the grain pile) and tuck herself under the covers. They're the same folks who'll tell you that the Song of Solomon is nothing more than a "theological metaphor referring to Christ and his bride." Ask 'em what they do with passages like "Your stature is like that of the palm, and your breasts like clusters of fruit. I said 'I will climb the palm tree; I will take hold of its fruit'" (Song 7:7–8). That's a Bible study, right?

No, I do not think Ruth and Boaz had sex that night; I do not think anything inappropriate happened at all. But this is no fellowship potluck, either. I'm telling you that the church has really crippled women when it tells them that their beauty is vain and they are at their feminine best when they are "serving others." A woman is at her best when she *is* being a woman. Boaz needs a little help getting going and Ruth has some options. She can badger him: All you do is work, work, work. Why won't you stand up and be a man? She can whine about it: Boaz, pleeease hurry up and marry me. She can emasculate him: I thought you were a real man; I guess I was wrong. Or she can use all she is as a woman to get him to use all he's got as a man. She can arouse, inspire, energize . . . Ask your man what he'd prefer.

Now, am I suggesting that a single woman spend the night at her boyfriend's apartment in order to arouse him to marry her? No. Am I saying that a married woman ought to offer herself sexually to her husband even though he's been abusive to her? No. No more than the story of Peter walking on the water tells us all to get a boat, go out on a lake, and give it a try. The *principle* of the story is what matters here. Ruth takes a risk—a risk every woman knows—when she makes herself vulnerable and alluring to Boaz. She arouses him to play the man. *She awakens his desire to be the Hero.* That's the point.

160

EMASCULATING WOMEN

Women pretty much fall into one of three categories: Dominating Women, Desolate Women, or Arousing Women. The first two are what happens to Eve as a result of the Fall. The third is a woman whose femininity is being restored by God and who offers it to others.

I mentioned Annie in *The Horse Whisperer* as an example of a dominating, emasculating woman. She needs nothing from her man. She has life under control. She wears the pants in the family. Her message is clear: "You are weak and untrustworthy. I am strong. Let me lead and things will go fine." The effect on a man is not good. When a woman becomes controlling and not in the least vulnerable, her seductiveness is shut down. The message is, "Back off—I'll handle this." Any wonder that he backs off?

So many women fear the wildness God put in their man. They are drawn to his strength, but then they set about taming him once they've "caught" him. "I don't want you riding a motorcycle anymore. I don't want you hanging around your friends so much. Why do you need to go off on all those adventures?" Women who make their husbands pee sitting down.

But there are other types of emasculating women. In the movie *Enchanted April*, we meet four women—two who are desolate and two who are emasculating. Caroline is a woman who is beautiful with the kind of beauty most women envy. But hers is a severe beauty. She uses it like a weapon to get what she wants, leaving a trail of broken hearts in her wake. There is nothing soft about her. Softness is key to a woman. Not weakness—softness. Tenderness. Mrs. Fisher, a wealthy widow, is the other emasculating character. She orders everyone around, runs her world like a dictator. She shows no emotion unless it is disgust in someone's apparent weakness. There is nothing alluring about her at all.

Emasculating women send a clear message: "I don't need you. I refuse to be vulnerable and inviting. You have nothing to offer me."

DESOLATE WOMEN

The third character in *Enchanted April* is Lottie. She is not harsh—just shut down from years of living with a selfish, domineering pig of a man. She looks like a whipped puppy, rushing to please him in any way, not out of love but out of fear and some weird idea of submission. She is depressed. Rose is Lottie's friend; they meet at church. She is the Religious Woman. The typical Church Lady. She's actually quite beautiful, but she dresses in such a way as to hide it. Bag-shaped dresses, hair in a bun. Her heart is also shut down. She hides behind her prayers and her "good works of service." She is weary and tired.

Desolate women don't seem at first pass to be all that emasculating. They don't attack or dominate. But neither do they allure. Their message is simply, "There's nothing here for you." The lights are off; they have dimmed their radiance; no one is home. A man in her presence feels . . . uninvited. Unwanted. It's a form of rejection, emasculation to be sure. But it's harder to point out because it's so subtle.

Desolate women can also be those whose ache is what *defines* them. Women who will do whatever it takes to get a man. The Woman at the Well in John 4 would be an example. She moves from lover to lover trying to fill the void within her. She's available—but in a clingy, desperate way. "Groveling," as one friend said, "manipulating, begging for attention." Like the character Catherine Zeta-Jones plays in *The Terminal*. Their message to men is, "I need you too much. Please tell me who I am. Fill me." Men use women like this—but they do not love them. They do not feel challenged to be a Hero. Desolate women do not call the men in their lives to be Heroes.

Arousing Women

If you would be loved, be loveable.
—Ovid

The beautiful story in *Enchanted April* is how each of the women actually becomes a woman indeed. Caroline softens, becomes tender and vulnerable. She no longer resents her beauty, but offers it gently, almost shyly, which for her is repentance. Lottie and Rose gain a sense of self. They become substantive, able to offer their men a real mate, not a doormat. They, too, become alluring; being *less* shy is repentance for them—no longer hiding but coming forward in a gentle way. The effect on the men in their lives is astounding. What severity and domineering and hiding and whining could not do, beauty does. Their men come forth as good men, repentant men. Heroes.

An arousing woman is one who calls forth the best in a man by offering who she is *as* a woman—someone who offers her beauty, her true heart, as we described in the last chapter. Such a stark contrast is set out in the movie *A Walk in the Clouds*. There are two women in Paul Sutton's life (played by Keanu Reeves). His wife is not an arousing woman. She pressures him: "You are not the man I want you to be." She is manipulating and demanding. Eventually she has an affair. The Hispanic woman he meets on the bus, however, is alluring. A strong and self-confident woman, she is also soft and inviting. Her message to him is, "You are an amazing man."

However it is expressed in the uniqueness of your own femininity, arousing Adam comes down to this:

Need him. And believe in him.

That is what a man needs to hear from his woman more than anything else. I need you. I need your strength. I believe in you. You have what it takes.

LOVING FALLEN MEN

Granted, not every man is on the road to redemption. There are men out there who are not safe and good men. Some of you are married to men like this. All of you will encounter them. How do you love them? With great wisdom and cunning. The last three chapters in Dan Allender's book *Bold Love* are "Loving an Evil Person," "Loving a Fool," and "Loving a Normal Sinner." You might find them helpful.

Jesus said, "Do not throw your pearls to pigs" (Matt. 7:6). By this we don't think he was calling some people pigs. He was saying, "Look—be careful that you do not give something precious to someone who, at best, cannot recognize its beauty, or at worst, will trample on it." Consider your feminine heart and beauty your treasure, your pearls. A woman can test and see if a man is willing to move in a good direction by offering a *taste* of what is available with her if he does. She does not give everything in a moment. As God does, she allures and waits to see what he will do. We'll try and offer a few examples.

Janice is married to a dull man. A man whose heart was so far buried she wondered if he was even there. Her anger and disappointment with him only drove him farther underground. He wasn't a violent man; to her knowledge he had no addictions. He was just—absent. Checked out as a human being. He was functioning but not passionate. A roommate but not a Lover, let alone a Hero. She decided to play Ruth.

One night when he came home, he found the children were off for a night at Grandma's. The table was set with a beautiful meal; candles were lit. (This is much like the story of Esther too.) Janice was wearing a beautiful blouse, discreetly *un*buttoned several buttons down. As the evening progressed, she unveiled the lace underwear she was wearing beneath. She invited him to make love. Now, what is important is what followed. The next night he came home,

hoping for a similar feast. When he moved toward her, she asked him softly why. He was a bit stunned by the question.

"Why do you want me? Is it only for my body—or are you pursuing my heart?" It was a brilliant trap, well set. He stumbled for an answer, but his intentions were exposed. "I long to give myself to you," she said, "but you need to give yourself to me. I want your heart in this marriage, not just your laundry." She awakened desire in him, but did not give herself to him that second night. She waited for him to move closer emotionally. It began an awkward but hopeful journey toward deeper intimacy.

Betsy was married to a verbally abusive man. An elder in the church, he looked great outside the home. But behind closed doors, he was just plain mean. She chose to keep her heart alive, to try and invite him to see what he was doing to her and how they might share something far better. She asked if he might see a counselor, which he did . . . until things got too close to home for him. Then he bailed.

She finally moved out—not seeking divorce, but as an invitation for him to feel the weight of the consequences of his life and his lack of repentance. She fasted and prayed. He did not choose to change, but laid the blame on her. He villainized her to their children, to his church. She held her ground. We're sad to say that he filed for divorce. She gave him many tastes of what life could be like together, if he would repent of his meanness. He chose not to. Like the story of Jesus with the rich young ruler, she let him walk away.

How generous and lavish God is with his beauty toward us. He sends the sun each day; he sends music and laughter and so many notes to our hearts. But he also says, "You will . . . find me when you seek me with all your heart" (Jer. 29:13). That is a good way for a woman to live as well. Not defiant, not hiding, but alluring and watching to see if he wants to come closer.

Now, we realize that many women need healing in their sexuality

Captivating

if they are going to enjoy sex with their spouse and live in wholeness as a sexual being. We have included a prayer for sexual healing in the appendix of this book. We hope you will find it *immensely* helpful.

SINGLE WOMEN

It might be encouraging to point out that Mary, Rahab, Ruth, and Tamar were all single women when the story of their greatness was told. (True, Mary was engaged, but she had reason to believe it wouldn't last long when she gave her "yes" to God.) They are such powerful reminders that this greatness, this beauty, can be lived out as a single woman. They also stand in stark contrast to some of the messages of "purity" given single women today. As one young woman wrote to us, "I am afraid that I and numerous other women have interpreted womanly purity as 'completely ignore the man you are interested in until he proposes to you.'"

And why, then, *would* he propose to you?

Of course a woman should be alluring to the man she is attracted to. A smile, a tenderness, an interest in him and his life are natural and welcome. To look your best; awaken him to your presence. Yes, you can offer beauty to him—in gently increasing amounts as he pursues and comes closer. And yes, there are parts of you that should be held as mysteries until he fully commits, and you offer yourself to him on your wedding night. Don't offer everything, but don't offer nothing.

How much, and when? That is more than we can say in a chapter. Walk with God. Be a wise and discerning woman. Be aware of the issues that could cause you to hold back or give too much. Be aware of the issues in him that could cause him to look to you for his validation or become paralyzed. Invite, arouse, and maintain your personal integrity.

166

There is an emotional promiscuity we've noticed among many good young men and women. The young man understands something of the journey of the heart. He wants to talk, to "share the journey." The woman is so grateful to be pursued, she opens up. They share the intimacies of their lives—their wounds, their walks with God. But he never commits. He enjoys her . . . then leaves. And she wonders, *What did I do wrong*? She failed to see his passivity. He really did not ever commit or offer assurances that he would. Like Willoughby to Marianne in *Sense and Sensibility*.

Be careful you do not offer too much of yourself to a man until you have good, solid evidence that he is a strong man willing to commit. Look at his track record with other women. Is there anything to be concerned about there? If so, bring it up. Also, does he have any close male friends—and what are *they* like as men? Can he hold down a job? Is he walking with God in a real and intimate way? Is he facing the wounds of his own life, and is he also demonstrating a desire to repent of Adam's passivity and/or violence? Is he headed somewhere with his life? A lot of questions, but your heart is a treasure, and we want you to offer it only to a man who is worthy and ready to handle it well.

GOOD MEN THAT DO NOT BELONG TO YOU

The way femininity can awaken masculine strength—and the way a good man's strength allows a woman to be beautiful—these can be offered in all sorts of holy ways between men and women who are not married to one another. Far too long we have lived in a culture of fear in the Church, fearing that any relationship between men and women will end in an affair. Sadly, we have forsaken so many opportunities to call one another forth with the grace of our genders.

John wasn't able to be present for our recent women's retreat. On the second day I had an encounter with an evil woman that left me shaken and under spiritual attack. I asked our colleague, a young man named Morgan, to pray for me. He did—fiercely. He rose up on my behalf and sent the Enemy packing. His prayers and his kind words to me allowed my heart to rest again and carry on through the day. I made myself vulnerable to him, needed him, in a perfectly innocent way. He came through for me, offered his strength in a perfectly innocent way. My thanks to him was a way of saying, "You have what it takes." Should that not be an encouragement to him?

In the same way, there are women in our fellowship who have offered to me (John) many words of encouragement, many tender kindnesses. They have spoken to me of how I have impacted their lives, touched their hearts, offered my strength on their behalf. And that has brought a great encouragement and inspiration to me— even at times when I felt I was failing Stasi as a man. But their encouragement and inspiration did not make me want to have an affair with them—it actually fueled my fire to go back and offer my strength *to* Stasi. It was a kind of affirmation that said, "You are a good man, a man of strength. As a woman I am grateful."

John has offered his strength and kind heart to many women in our community—listened to their lives, helped them find their way, fought fiercely for many of them. His strong, kind presence awakens their beauty. In some sense it is God saying to them, "This is available—not here, in John—but this kind of man is available. Doesn't that awaken your heart as a woman?"

There are all sorts of opportunities in our lives for this. Truth be told, it will be unavoidable. As a man comes alive, the women in his world will experience and enjoy his strength, the power of his masculine presence. As a woman comes alive, the men in her world will experience and enjoy her beauty, the richness of her feminine presence. Yes—this exchange of strength and beauty will be a test of character. When something is awakened in us by another man or woman, we do have a choice in that moment. We choose to accept the awakening as an invitation to go find that with *our* man or woman. Or to pray, if we are single, that this sort of man or woman will come to us from God's hand. We will *have* to face this kind of test as we relate to members of the opposite sex. The only other option is to veil ourselves—as the Muslims insist their women do. A sad and unbiblical way to live.

Remember our answer to the question, "How do I love a man?" Entice him. The sexual connotation of "entice" may have some of you struggling still with all those situations in which sexual intimacy is not appropriate. We mean it as a principle, a picture of how femininity can arouse masculinity in many, many ways. Perhaps you have heard the old story, attributed to Aesop, about the argument between the North Wind and the Sun. It might help you get past your concern.

> The North Wind and the Sun had an argument one day. They disputed which of them was the stronger. A traveler came along the road at that time, and the Sun suggested a way to resolve the argument. Whoever was able to cause the traveler to remove his coat would be the stronger. The Wind accepted the challenge and the Sun hid himself behind a cloud. The Wind began to blow. Yet the harder he blew, the more the traveler clutched his coat about himself. The Wind sent rain, even hail. The traveler clung even more desperately to his coat. Finally, in despair, the Wind gave up. The Sun came out and began to shine in all his glory upon the traveler. Quite soon the man had removed his coat. "How did you do that?" asked the Wind. "It was easy," said the Sun, "I lit the day. Through gentleness I got my way." ("The North Wind and the Sun")

CHAPTER TEN

Mothers, Daughters, Sisters

❧

Adam named his wife Eve, because she would
become the mother of all the living.
—GENESIS 3:20

How wide and sweet and wild motherhood—
and sisterhood—can be.
—REBECCA WELLS

We have our mother tongue, which is our native language. We have mother earth from which all growing things come, and Mother Nature, the unpredictable source of typhoons and tornadoes. The mother lode is the source of riches and a "mother headache" is one that sends you to bed. The mother of all storms is fierce, and the motherland is the home we left and long for. Mother is the source of life. Mother is powerful. Mother is strong. Mother can nurture, and mother can destroy. Depending on our experiences, the word *mother* can evoke images of a warm, welcoming woman or turn our blood to ice.

Whether good or bad, whether redemptive or destructive, our relationships with our mothers affected us to the core of our beings, helping to shape us into the women we have become. As Dinah says in *The Red Tent*, "If you want to understand any woman you must first ask about her mother and then listen carefully."

We are not all mothers, but we all had one. Or longed for one. The relationship between a mother and daughter is a holy, tender, fierce thing fraught with land mines and umbilical cords that stretch and sometimes strangle. The desire in a daughter to please her mother is matched only by her desire to be separate from her. Most mother/daughter relationships go through a stormy season during the girl's adolescence. Hormones rage and the brunt of the raging often lands on the mom. Words are flung, accusations aimed at the heart. "You're not going to wear *that*, are you?" has been uttered by many a mother in horror as her daughter is getting ready to go out. "You don't even know what you're talking about!" has been slung by many a daughter. The way a mother weathers this stormy season of her daughter's transition from girlhood to womanhood can affect their relationship for the rest of their lives.

Many a good woman makes the desperate mistake of believing that her daughter is a reflection of herself, an extension of herself, and therefore the verdict on her as a mother and as a woman. She is dumbfounded, disappointed, sometimes wounded deeply when her "little girl" makes choices wholly foreign to what she would have chosen. The result of entangling the verdict on yourself as a woman with your daughter's life is deep wounding and a further twisting of the relationship. The mother will try and set things right; the daughter will pull away even further to establish her own identity.

Mothers rightly teach their daughters how to behave and what to believe. The decision to continue to hold to what has been taught belongs to the daughter when she comes into her own. A mother hopes that her daughter's coming into her own is a passage to celebrate. But often it takes years for a mother and daughter to reconcile their differences—let alone enjoy them.

Girls' hearts flourish in homes where they are *seen* and *invited* to become ever more themselves. Parents who enjoy their daughters are giving them and the world a great gift. Mothers in particular have the opportunity to offer encouragement to their daughters by inviting them into their feminine world and by treasuring their daughters' unique beauty.

I don't know what it is like to have a daughter. I missed that. My husband and my sons are outside right now blowing things up. They're taking M-60s apart and combining all the gunpowder to make really big explosions. Tea parties don't happen here. No one lets me brush their hair. But although I don't have a daughter, I am one.

THE LONG ROAD HOME

My relationship with my mother was strained. It was painful. For both of us. Our communication was fraught with hidden meanings and misunderstandings. Remember the messages of the wounds I received? She was grieved to have learned she was having another child, and that child happened to be me. I felt I was a disappointment to her in what I believed, how I dressed, what I thought, and who I was. It wasn't until I was forty-one years old that I realized I made her feel exactly the same way.

You remember my story growing up—how my mother was overwhelmed by my coming along. I was too much for her, and so I did my best to hide my true self and be the easy daughter she needed me to be. I longed for her to want to know me, to want to play with me. I loved kissing her cheek good night and inhaling deeply the fragrance of her night cream (something I continued into adulthood). I mentioned earlier that I used to pretend to be sick, because then I got her attention. She'd give me books and read to me and bring me meals in bed. A high fever meant her love was coming along with 7 UP and vanilla ice cream. (It is no fun, by the way, being sick with John. He brings me enormous vitamins and horrible-tasting, good-for-me green drinks.)

In elementary school, my sister ingeniously told my mother that her teacher required my mom to read to her every night to help her with her education. A story she made up, but one that brought the desired results of snuggling with my mom and having her undivided attention for a full twenty minutes. We do what we can.

When my mother found out that I was smoking in the fifth grade, she sadly said that I wasn't her little girl anymore. I cried. And I got better at hiding. She didn't know my dreams, my struggles, my gifts, or the treacherous path my life was taking. Throughout junior high, high school, and college, I appeared to be a good student who made no waves. Beneath the surface, I was seeking affirmation and life in all the worldly, destructive ways available. I felt unloved, unwanted, and abandoned—worthless, really. The choices I made from that place brought death to my own soul and death to others as I slid ever more deeply into despair, both hating and hiding myself.

When I came home blasted one night in high school after having been sick all over myself and left my soiled clothes in the tub, neither my mother nor my dad said a word. Nor did they confront me later when I came home too drunk to get into the house without their help. Being arrested for drunk driving cost me driving privileges for two weeks, but that was the end of it. One night I simply didn't come home at all. When I finally showed up in the morning, I was met by a hysterical mother who had, during my absence, smashed all the drug paraphernalia I openly kept in my room. In her frantic worry to find me, she had looked through my school notebook to find my friend's phone number. What she found instead was a list of all the drugs I had taken in the last month. It was a very long list.

I loved my mom. I didn't want her to know about the drugs. I did not want to hurt her. Yes, she failed me. All mothers fail their children to varying degrees. But she also loved me. That was what was *most* true. I was shamed by her discovery. But I did not repent. No. Not yet. Instead, I tried to become even better at hiding.

I was sexually promiscuous during my college years . . . searching for the elusive feeling of being wanted, of being thought beautiful. My mother was a strong Catholic and often wondered aloud about people who had done things I had done, seriously questioning if God could ever forgive them, wondering how they could live with themselves. I took in her condemning words as blows while silently hoping God could forgive me, that I could forgive me.

By the grace and to the glory of God, I became a Christian my last year in college. Jesus quite literally saved me. But I wasn't a Catholic anymore. Or at least, I wasn't *pretending* to be a Catholic anymore. (I faked it through high school.) I was now attending a nondenominational church.

My mom was glad that I stopped doing drugs. (We pretended she didn't know about any of the sexual sin.) She was glad that I was praying again. But she was deeply grieved that I wasn't going to her church. When we would broach the subject of faith, both of our defenses rose like battlements. We couldn't see each other over them, let alone hear what the other was saying. Instead of being a shared joy, our doctrinal differences became a barbed-wire fence we could not cross.

So we talked about the weather. For fifteen years.

I read a story recently about a young woman who had just given birth to her first child, and her own mother had come to help care for her. The baby had kept the new mother up most of the night with his little mysterious noises, so she was going to ask her mom how long it was before you stopped hearing all those sounds. Before she could ask, however, her own mother asked her, "Are you getting a cold, dear? I thought I heard you wheezing last night." No matter how old your children become, they are still your children. Just as it is true that no matter how old you are when your parents die, you are still an orphan.

I don't know exactly when a softening began to occur between my mother and me, but slowly we became more graceful with each other. I do know that it began after I had looked honestly at my childhood and grieved deeply the wounds my parents had dealt me, inflicted by action as well as inaction. I had looked squarely at my youth. I'd been angry. I'd been sorrowful. And after a season, I was able to forgive. I began to see my mother with new eyes.

My mother and I began to enjoy, even celebrate, our shared faith in God, and not debate the differences. From out of the blue one day, my mom apologized to me for missing me, ignoring my questions, and turning a blind eye to my struggles while I was growing up. I began to understand that in those years she had been treading water with all that she had just to stay afloat.

OUR LAST YEAR TOGETHER

In the photograph by my bed my mother is perpetually smiling on me. I guess I have forgiven us both, although sometimes in the night my dreams will take me back to the sadness, and I have to wake up and forgive us again. (Lily in *The Secret Life of Bees* by Sue Monk Kidd)

Years later, as God addressed yet another layer of unhealed wounds, I was grieving that in my mother's presence I still felt "not good enough." I still felt like a failure to her, a deep disappointment. Her words continued to pierce. It was then that God showed me that the way my mother made me feel was exactly the way *I made her feel.* A disappointment. An embarrassment. A failure. And in that moment, I knew with utter clarity that it was true. I felt her sorrow. I saw some of her irritating comments to me in a new light. She wanted me to like her, know her, and enjoy her just as much as I wanted her to feel that way about me. And I had withheld my acceptance from her. I realized for the first time how deeply I had wounded her.

I was compelled by God to see her as soon as possible. I was able to make all the arrangements, get on a plane within days, and fly to see my mother so that I could apologize to her in person. We sat at her kitchen table and I offered her, perhaps for the first time, my true heart. I told her that I knew I had made her feel not good enough. I knew that I made her feel that she was a disappointment to me. I told her that I was deeply sorry, that it simply was not true. I loved who she was. I was proud of her. I was glad she was my mom. And I asked her to forgive me.

She couldn't speak. She didn't have to. But I understood by her eyes, through her shy expression and her tender countenance, that she did forgive me. We embraced then with nothing in between.

How can I relate to you the spacious place in our souls that act of repentance and forgiveness created for us? The walls, the barriers, came down. We could offer and receive each other's love and acceptance and enjoyment for the first time in our lives. We spent the rest of that evening looking over old family albums. Nestled up next to my mother, I heard her say, "Look how precious you are." Pointing at pictures of a very young Stasi, she said, "You were always so adorable!" It was a tender time. A healing time. A time that was true and real and full of love.

It was also the last time we had together before she was diagnosed with multiple myeloma. A short month after our relationship's restoration, Mom felt like she was dying. She told her doctor the same, and he ordered some tests. The tests revealed that her kidneys were failing. The cancer was extremely advanced. She was right. She was dying. My mom and I had four more months together where we loved each other unconditionally and fully. How I wanted to have years together in this new place, and yet, how utterly grateful I am to have had the time at all.

God restored much to us in those months. I am weeping now as I remember. Those times, those memories, are gold to me.

THE COST

It is one thing to suffer. It is something far worse to walk alongside one you love who is suffering intensely and be unable to do anything about it. Many of you have lived this. You know. When I was six years old, I nearly cut my finger off in a slamming door. When the doctor was shooting the painkiller directly into my wound, I looked up at my mother through my streaming tears and heard her say that it was hurting her far worse than it was hurting me. I didn't understand her then, but I do now.

During her illness, while I was visiting to take care of her, she looked at me and tenderly said, "I'm sorry. I'm sorry to be putting you through this." Here she is, suffering, dying, in pain, unable to eat or even swallow, and she is sorry for *me*; she is sorry to be the cause of suffering in my heart. She would gladly have borne it herself and spared me the sorrow, spared me the pain of bearing her pain, her loss.

I have heard it said that having a child is like having your heart walk around outside of your body. How a mother aches to protect her child. And yet all the while, from infancy to adulthood, a good mother is training her child to move ever more away from her, to need her less and less. Mothers love and long for their children. Their hearts ache for them, over them. A woman bleeds when she gives birth, but that is only the beginning of the bleeding. A heart enlarged by all a mother endures with and through her child's life;

all a mother prays and works and hopes for on her child's behalf bleeds too.

A mother's heart is a vast and glorious thing. My mother's heart was expansive, having been enlarged by suffering and years of clinging to Jesus while being misunderstood, dismissed, and judged by those she loved most. Me included. It had cost her to love, had cost her much to mother. It always does. But she would tell you that it's worth it, that there is no other way.

The last time my mother was able to walk to the bathroom, I helped hold her from the front while her sister held her from behind. On the way back, Mom had to take several stops to rest, walking a few inches at a time. At her last resting stop, I looked down into her eyes and said, "Well, what a great opportunity to hug you!" I hugged her, lingering with her frail frame in my arms and then looked into her sky blue eyes. In those eyes, I saw the depth of my mother's love for me. It was measureless, vast, unconditional, tender, deep, strong, joyful, and clear. You could dive into eyes like that; get lost in that kind of love. Or be found.

Finally I understood. My mother loved me. She had loved me during those years; I just hadn't seen it. There was grace in her eyes and a knowing that all was well, that all would be well. And that nothing was lost. Not in our years of missing one another and not in the years that I am left missing her now.

Both my parents are gone now, off and away and fully alive in heaven. I tell you this story because I want you to know that redemption is possible. Healing is possible. Ask Jesus to bring it to you and yours. Then, if you can, go, call your mother. Tell her you love her.

To Mother

As large as the role is that our mothers play, the word *mother* is more powerful when used as a verb than as a noun. All women are not mothers, but all women are called *to mother*. To mother is to nurture, to train, to educate, to rear. As daughters of Eve, all women are uniquely gifted to help others in their lives become more of who they truly are—*to encourage, nurture, and mother them toward their true selves*. In doing this, women partner with Christ in the vital mission of bringing forth life.

"Train a child in the way he should go, and when he is old he will not depart from it" (Prov. 22:6 NKJV). This verse is not a promise about faith. It is not speaking of training a child to follow Christ or promising that if you do, the grown child will continue to follow him. Sorry. The proverb is about raising a child to know who he is and to guide him in becoming ever more himself. *In the way he should go.* Not in the way you would like him to go in order to validate you as a mother and a woman. It speaks of teaching a child to live from his heart, attuned to it, awake to it, aware of it, and when that child is grown he will continue to live a life from the heart. *It is about seeing who a person really is and calling him out to be that person.*

The impact on a life that has been seen and called out is dramatic and eternal. The nurturing of life is a high and holy calling. And as a woman, it is yours. Yes, it takes many shapes and has a myriad of faces. Yes, men are called to this as well. But uniquely and deeply, this calling makes up part of the very fiber of a woman's soul—the calling to mother.

I am reminded of a courageous African-American woman who was thrilled to purchase her first home. After moving in, she came home from work to find drug dealers doing business on her front steps. It seems her new home was smack dab in the center of their "territory" in Los Angeles. She wouldn't stand for it. Head held high, finger wagging, she "mothered" them to higher aims. She mothered them out of their sin. She mothered them into becoming the young men they were meant to become.

You can mother other people's children. In truth, our world needs you to. My friend Lori's house was the center of activity while her girls were still in school. Their friends loved to hang out at her house. She offered them life. She counseled them. She encouraged them. She mothered them with love and strength. She also baked them fabulous treats. She has played and continues to play a major role in many young women's lives, impacting them for good, calling them forth to become who they are meant to be. We think of a woman C. S. Lewis describes meeting in heaven in his book *The Great Divorce*. A Teacher is showing him around the place when they encounter a woman of stunning beauty.

"It's someone ye'll never have heard of. Her name on earth was Sarah Smith and she lived at Golders Green."

"She seems to be . . . well, a person of particular importance?"

"Aye. She is one of the great ones. Ye have heard that fame in this country and fame on earth are two quite different things."

". . . And who are all these young men and women on each side?"

"They are her sons and daughters."

"She must have had a very large family, Sir."

"Every young man or boy that met her became her son— even if it was only the boy that brought the meat to her back door. Every girl that met her was her daughter."

"Isn't that a bit hard on their own parents?"

"No. There *are* those that steal other people's children. But her motherhood was of a different kind. Those on whom it fell went back to their natural parents loving them more. Few men looked on her without becoming, in a certain fashion, her lovers. But it was the kind of love that made them not less true, but truer, to their own wives."

We mother each other when we offer our concern, our care, our comfort. We mother each other when we see a need and rise to meet it, whether it is a sweater for a friend who is chilly, a meal for a struggling family, or a listening ear for a friend who is hurting.

All women are called to mother. And all women are called to give birth. Women give birth to all kinds of things—to books (it's nearly as hard as a child, believe me), to churches, to movements. Women give birth to ideas, to creative expressions, to ministries. We birth life in others by inviting them into deeper realms of healing, to deeper walks with God, to deeper intimacy with Jesus. A woman is not less of a woman because she is not a wife or has not physically borne a child. The heart and life of a woman is much more vast than that. All women are made in the image of God in that we bring forth life. When we enter into our world and into the lives of those we love and offer our tender and strong feminine hearts, we cannot help but mother them.

My Sister, My Friend

I love the way women friends have with each other. When I gather with a group of women friends, inevitably someone begins to rub someone else's back. Hair gets played with. Merciful, tender, caressing, healing touches are given. Men don't do this with each other. It is unique to women. When women gather, they ask meaningful questions. They want to know how you *are*. Recipe swapping is all well and good, gardening hints helpful, but women friends unabashedly dive into matters of the heart.

My mom mothered me. But she isn't the only woman who has. My sisters certainly did. Some of my elementary school teachers did. My neighbors did. These days I receive it from the gentle, tender acts of kindness offered to me from the friends God has given me. The gift of friendship among women is a treasure not to be

taken lightly. Women friends become the face of God to one another—the face of grace, of delight, of mercy.

The capacity of a woman's heart for meaningful relationships is vast. There is no way your husband or your children can ever provide the intimacy and relational satisfaction you need. A woman *must* have women friends.

It is here, in the realm of relationship, that women receive the most joy and the profoundest sorrows. The friendships of women inhabit a terrain of great mystery. Movies like *Beaches* or *Fried Green Tomatoes* or *Steel Magnolias* try to capture this. In these movies the friendships endure testing and trial; they deepen and they last. The men in the lives of these women may leave, but their girlfriends do not. Although often quoted in weddings, Ruth was speaking to a woman when she said, "Where you go I will go, and where you stay I will stay. Your people will be my people and your God my God" (Ruth 1:16). There is a fierce jealousy, a fiery devotion, and a great loyalty between women friends. Our friendships flow in the deep waters of the heart where God dwells and transformation takes place. It is here, in this holy place, that a woman can partner with God in impacting another and *be impacted* by another for lasting good. It is here that she can mother, nurture, encourage, and call forth Life.

Little girls have best friends. Grown women long for them. To have a woman friend is to relax into another soul and be welcomed in all that you are and all that you are not. To know that as a woman, you are not alone. Friendships between women provide a safe place to share in the experiences of life *as a woman*. Who but another woman can fully understand PAP smears and mammograms, PMS, the longing to bear a child, and living in a world that feels run by men? It is a great gift to know that you see as another sees, an immense pleasure to be understood, to enjoy the easy companionship of one you can let your guard down with.

Friendship is a great gift. One to be prayed for and not taken for granted. If you do not have the kind of friendship you long for, ask God to bring it into your life, to give you eyes to recognize it when he does. When God gives a friend, he is entrusting us with the care of another's heart. It is a chance to mother and to sister, to be a Life giver, to help someone else become the woman she was created to be, to walk alongside her and call her deep heart forth.

Friendships need to be nurtured and guarded and fought for. We need to call one another without waiting to be called first. We need to ask how our friends are doing and really listen to their answers. Listen between the lines. We love our friends by *pursuing* them—calls, little presents, cards, invitations to play, to go for a walk, to go to a movie. We offer our hearts.

My friend Dena realized a few years ago that I liked presents. When I'm out and about, I'll often see a little something that I think a friend would like, so I pick it up and surprise her with it. Small things. Simple things. So Dena started giving me little presents. I loved it! Then I clued in that for Dena, what she liked best wasn't presents at all but the gift of time—the most treasured of all commodities. I still give her little presents every now and again. I can't help it. But when I'm able, I give her hours.

We need to pay attention to each other, really *see* one another. That truly is the greatest gift.

AWKWARD LOVE

And let me say clearly, true friendship is *opposed*.

One woman often feels less important to the other, or accused or needy or misunderstood. Honest communication in love is the only way to live and grow in friendships. There are ebbs and flows. There may be too much dependence. There may be real hurt and disappointment. In fact, it's inevitable in our broken world. But with the grace of God firmly holding us, reminding us that he is the source of our true happiness, it is possible to nurture and sustain deep friendships throughout our lives. We are not made to live our lives alone. We are designed to live in relationship and share in the lives of other women. We need each other. God knows that. He will help us. We have only to ask and surrender, to wait, to hope, and in faith to love. We must also repent.

For a woman to enjoy relationship, she must repent of her need to control and her insistence that people fill her. Fallen Eve demands that people "come through" for her. Redeemed Eve is being met in the depths of her soul by Christ and is free to offer to others, free to desire, and willing to be disappointed. Fallen Eve has been wounded by others and withdraws in order to protect herself from further harm. Redeemed Eve knows that she has something of value to offer; that she is made for relationship. Therefore, being safe and secure in her relationship with her Lord, she can risk being vulnerable with others and offer her true self.

> To love at all is to be vulnerable. Love anything, and your heart will certainly be wrung and possibly broken. If you want to make sure of keeping it intact, you must give your heart to no one, not even to an animal. Wrap it careful round with hobbies and little luxuries; avoid all entanglements; lock it up safe in the casket or coffin of your selfishness. But in that casket—safe, dark, motionless, airless—it will change. It will not be broken; it will become unbreakable, impenetrable, irredeemable . . . The only place outside Heaven where you can be perfectly safe from all the dangers . . . of love is Hell. (C. S. Lewis, *The Four Loves*)

In your friendships, in all your relationships, you will disappoint others and they will disappoint you. That comes with the territory of being human. But it is not the truest thing. In your relationships, you have the opportunity to practice loving; to partner with God in mothering, in bringing forth life in another and having your heart enlarged by caring for another and your life enriched by sharing the adventure that life is.

AN OPEN HAND

Do you remember that old Chinese proverb "If you love something, set it free. If it comes back to you, it's yours. If it doesn't, it never was"? It is true for friendships. Studies reveal that most friendships undergo a transition every five years. People change. People grow. At least we want to. That said, though sharing a part of a person's journey is wonderful, it doesn't mean that we will share all of their journey, nor they ours. Most friendships are for a *season*. I have damaged dear friendships by expecting them not to change. My expectation of intimacy in friendship began to feel like demand to those I so wanted in my life but whom God was calling in a different direction. Friendships are messy. Misunderstandings can run rampant and if unchecked will lead to death. Remember, godly relationships are *opposed*. If you want your friendships to last, you will need to have the occasional hard conversation. Honesty is our friend, dear ones. Hiding how we feel, what we experience and come to believe about a person is not. These days I am learning to love better those God brings into my life and yet hold them with an open hand.

Perhaps it would be good to say just a few words about circles of intimacy. Jesus had them, and so do we. Jesus had the Twelve, but he also had the three. Peter and the sons of Zebedee were with him at the Mount of Transfiguration and were also invited by him to stay awake and pray in the Garden of Gethsemane. (You remember that they failed him there. Jesus understands well that friends disappoint . . . yet he continues to love.) You can only have one, two, maybe three intimate friends in your life at any given time. That's just the way of the heart.

There is room for more dear friends, but they are a little further out, in the next circle, like Jesus' Twelve. Close, but not the ones you would call in need in the middle of the night. And then there are your acquaintances, loose friendships, as Jesus had in the other disciples. It is natural and good to have circles of friendship. Friends will move from one circle to the other, but you can't possibly sustain intimacy with everyone. That said, you also don't want to have intimacy with no one. Jesus desires it with us, and he understands that we need it with others as well. He made us that way.

God invites us to risk trusting him and enter into redemptive friendships with others—to open ourselves up to the possibility of being hurt as well as to the possibility of tasting the sweet fruit of companionship. Yet, no matter how wonderful a taste of relational fullness you have, you will want more. If you had an amazing connection yesterday with someone, when you wake this morning, you will want it again. Eve possesses a bottomless well of longing. Jesus alone, our Truest Friend (John 15:15), is the never-ending fount, which can slake her thirst. No other source, no other relationship will fully satisfy. God made us that way. On purpose.

Deep longing is part of the grace given to Eve to drive her to the River of Life.

While our hearts drink deeply and rest in God's good heart, he "mothers" us so that we continue to become ever more truly who he intends us and created us to be—the women we truly are. A woman who partners with God in bringing forth life in this damaged world—offering, loving, inviting others to become who they were meant to be—she is a mother indeed. She—like God—offers Freedom and Life.

* MOTHERS, DAUGHTERS, SISTERS

Oh gently lay your head
Upon My chest
And I will comfort you like a Mother while you rest.
The tide can change so fast
But I will stay
The same through Past, the same in Future,
Same Today.

Oh weary, tired and worn
Let out your sighs
And drop that heavy load you hold
Cuz Mine is light.
I know you through and through
There's no need to hide.
I want to show you love that is deep and high and wide.

For I am constant.
I am near.
I am peace that shatters all your secret fears.
I am holy.
I am wise.
I'm the only One, who knows your heart's desires.

Oh gently lay your head upon My chest
And I will comfort you like a Mother
While you rest.
—JILL PHILLIPS, "I AM"

CHAPTER ELEVEN

Warrior Princesses

"Me, a princess?"
"You are the legal heir."
"I never lead anyone."
"We will help you to be a princess, to rule. If you refuse to accept
the throne then the kingdom will cease to exist as we know it."
—*THE PRINCESS DIARIES*

In God's name, we must fight them!
—JOAN OF ARC

*W*omen are often portrayed in stories and tales as the Damsel in Distress. We are the ones for whom men rise up and slay dragons. We are the "weaker sex," said to faint at the sight of blood, needing to be spared the gory details of battle whether on the field or in the marketplace. We are the ones waiting in our flowing gowns for the knight to come and carry us away on the back of his white horse. And yes, there are days when a knight in shining armor would be most welcome. We do long to be fought for; loved enough to be courageously protected. But there is a mighty strength and fierceness set in the hearts of women by God. This fierceness is true to who we are and what we are created to do.

Women are warriors too.

There is an old tale of an invasion against the Vikings, who were the first Europeans to explore North America and settle here some seven hundred years ago. Gail Collins writes in *America's Women,* "When the Viking camp was attacked by Indians, causing the male defenders to flee, a pregnant Freydis grabbed a handy weapon, took out her swollen breasts, 'and whetted the sword upon them' according to a Viking chronicler. The sight of her so unnerved the war party they 'became afraid and ran away.'" What a woman!

I've already told you that when I was a little girl I used to love World War II movies. How I longed to be a part of them. Not the movies themselves, but the real thing. I wanted to be part of something noble and grand and heroic and good. Didn't you? I am not alone in that deep longing. During the Civil War, more than four hundred women disguised themselves as men so that they, too, could fight alongside their husbands, fathers, and sons. History is laden with stories of women rising up to defend their families, their land, their honor.

In the mythic story *The Return of the King,* Éowyn, battle maiden of the Rohirrim, disguises herself as a man and rides to war, joining her kinsmen in the greatest battle of her time. She rides beautifully, and she handles a sword with deadly skill. In the thick of the battle, she fights heroically. Tragically, her uncle the king is attacked by the leader of the enemy's army, and as he swoops down to finish the king off, Éowyn steps in to block his path. She will not allow her uncle even to be touched by the evil wraith.

"Begone, foul dwimmerlaik, lord of carrion! Leave the dead in peace!"

A cold voice answered: "Come not between the Nazgûl and his prey! Or he will not slay thee in thy turn. He will bear thee away to the houses of lamentation, beyond all darkness, where thy flesh shall be devoured, and thy shriveled mind be left naked to the Lidless Eye."

A sword rang as it was drawn. "Do what you will; but I will hinder it, if I may."

In the battle that follows, the wraith is assured, cocky even. His strength is greater, his weapons more deadly. He boasts of an ancient prophecy, proclaiming, "*Thou fool. No living man may hinder me!*" And it is here that Éowyn is finally and fully victorious.

> It seemed that Dernhelm [Éowyn] laughed, and the clear voice was like the ring of steel. "But no living man am I! You look upon a woman. Éowyn I am, Éomund's daughter . . . Begone, if you be not deathless! For living or dark undead, I will smite you, if you touch him."

Éowyn removes her helmet and lets her hair fall free. She declares herself "no man" and fighting *as a woman*, slays her enemy. Something critically important is revealed in this story. Women are called to join in the Greatest Battle of all time—the battle being waged for the hearts of those around us. The human heart is the battlefield. The war is a deadly one; the results devastating or glorious, but always eternal. We are needed. There is much to be done. The hour is late. But we will only be victorious when we enter in with our feminine hearts—*when we battle as women.*

Redeemed women of God have tender, merciful hearts, back-bones of steel, and hands that have been trained for battle. There is something incredibly fierce in the heart of a woman that is to be contended with—not dismissed, not disdained, but recognized, honored, welcomed, and trained.

FIGHTING BACK

"There is a strength in you. I see it."
—WILLIAM WALLACE TO THE PRINCESS IN *BRAVEHEART*

About eleven years ago, John brought home a book by Neil Anderson. I think it was *The Bondage Breaker*. John had begun to encounter spiritual warfare issues in some of the folks he was counseling and wanted to learn a little more about it. Curious, I opened the book and began to read some of the case histories Dr. Anderson writes about. One in particular caught my attention. He described a woman who was often dizzy. The feeling of dizziness would frequently come upon her and throw her off balance both physically and spiritually. *Huh*, I thought. *I get dizzy a lot too.* I mentioned this to John, and he was totally surprised. He never knew this about me. It was something I had lived with or under for years, but it never occurred to me to tell him about it. To me, it was normal.

It's amazing what we will live with because we think it's normal when it is *not*.

So we decided to perform an experiment. The next time a wave of dizziness came over me, I would command it in the name of Jesus to depart from me and see what happened. I didn't have to wait long. The next day I was busy with the activities of my daily life and suddenly, out of nowhere, I got hit with dizziness. I prayed and commanded the dizziness to leave in the authority of Jesus' name. And guess what? It left! Immediately. I was stunned. The next wave came later, and I prayed again. Again it left. Whoa! Something was going on here that was completely foreign to me. A whole new dimension of Christianity opened up for me. The dizziness was a form of spiritual attack. That whole Ephesians passage about putting on the armor of God . . . he meant it. We would need it.

The dizzy spells (interesting phrase) did not cease quickly. In fact, they increased, both in number and intensity. I had to learn to stand and to keep standing, "resist him, standing firm in the faith," as Peter urged (1 Peter 5:9). I had to learn in a new way to "not grow weary in doing good" (2 Thess. 3:13 NKJV), and to "pray without ceasing"

(1 Thess. 5:17 NKJV). It was as if the assaulting spirit(s) didn't believe I would stand firm against them and so they kept trying.

I got hit a few weeks later with a wave of dizziness that knocked me off my feet. From the ground, I prayed again, commanding it to leave me in the name of Jesus Christ. It did. And I have never been assaulted by dizziness again. Something that I had lived with for decades is now gone, for good. Through the experience of standing firm against the attack of dizziness, God had begun to train my hands and my heart for battle.

EMOTIONAL ATTACKS

I saw, in gradual vision through my tears,
The sweet, sad years, the melancholy years,
Those of my own life, who by turns had flung
A shadow across me.
—ELIZABETH BARRETT BROWNING

I (Stasi) have struggled with depression for most of my life. Even as a child, depression and suicidal thoughts plagued me. You remember, I tried to end my life when I was just ten years old. My spirit was weighed down. After our second child was born, I felt lost at sea. I was filled with self-doubt, anger, shame, and a deep sense of worthlessness. I loved my husband. I loved my sons. But I was keenly aware that I was not able to love them well. I wanted to be happy. But I was not. I was disconnected from my heart and from my God. I had no clue why I felt the way I did, other than believing that there was something deeply wrong with me and there always would be.

When we moved to Colorado Springs, I wanted to volunteer at the local Crisis Pregnancy Center. I wanted to be a counselor who did the pregnancy testing and met with the young women. The issues surrounding an unwanted pregnancy and the choices a girl feels forced to make are something I was and remain passionate about. You see, I had an abortion when I was in high school. I felt as if a part of my soul died along with my unborn child that day, and I wanted to help women not make the same grievous decision.

It turned out, however, that the center didn't allow women who'd had previous abortions to counsel others until they went through a class called "Post Abortion Counseling and Education." They wisely offered this path of healing to women, required it even for their volunteers. Okay. So I went.

It was incredible. I hadn't told many people about my past, and now here I was in a room with ten or so other women, exposing my shame. All of the other women were Christians—repentant and brokenhearted. Most were working in ministry positions. All of them had had at least one abortion; some had had many. And all of us needed the forgiveness and deep healing work of God.

God used that group to lance my heart. The nature of the group was such that we dealt only with the issue of abortion in our lives. If the process caused other painful issues to surface, we needed to seek additional counseling elsewhere. It was not long before I was on the phone to the leader, asking her for a referral. Other issues were not only stirred up, I was reeling in excruciating pain. I began to look at my life and consider for the first time that the sorrows and abuses I had received possibly were not all my fault or merely what I deserved.

Counseling began. God brought me to a wonderful, insightful, lovely Christian woman who honored my soul and invited me to take a deeper look. She walked with me, with God, into the dungeons of my heart and helped me to see that Christ had destroyed the iron gates. I met with Laura for quite a while before I hit a place in my life where I couldn't make any progress. I couldn't think clearly. I didn't have the energy or the hope to go further. It was then that she suggested I begin taking antidepressants.

My father was a manic-depressive. They call it bipolar now. Chemical imbalances get passed down. (Thanks, Dad.) So I started taking the medicine. Within a couple of weeks, I no longer felt the weight over my soul that I had lived with the majority of my life. I wondered, *Is this what other people feel like all the time? Sheesh!* I could now move forward with God into deeper realms of my heart. The sky became blue. Life was no longer altogether too much.

Antidepressants are stigmatized in the church. Some call them "happy pills." Others say that if you are filled with the Holy Spirit and walking with God in faith, you will not need them. They shame those who are responsibly taking them. But we don't shame diabetics who need to take insulin. Why do we shame people with a chemical imbalance who need to take something to help them? Once my father began taking lithium, he no longer had the dramatic mood swings that were the bane of our lives, and he became a much better man, more of the man he truly was. There is no shame in needing to take medicine whether to help in a short, difficult period or for the bulk of your life.

We human beings are made up of three interwoven parts. As Paul says, "May God himself . . . sanctify you through and through. May your whole spirit, soul and body be kept blameless at the coming of our Lord Jesus Christ" (1 Thess. 5:23). We are body, soul, and spirit. Each part affects the others in a mysterious interplay of life. By seeking healing through counseling, God was addressing my soul. God's provision of antidepressants was a tremendous help to my body. I made real progress. But it was not enough. God wanted me to engage my spirit.

A foul spirit of depression had its bloody claws in my life. It often works like that—the Enemy knows our weaknesses, and he preys upon them. Demons smell human brokenness like sharks smell blood in the water, and they move in to take advantage of the weakened soul. Paul warns about this in Ephesians when, *writing to*

Christians, he warns us not to "give the devil a foothold" in our lives through unhealed and mishandled emotions (4:26–27). God had me begin to stand against it.

James and Peter both exhort us to *resist* our Enemy (James 4:7; 1 Peter 5:8–9). Jesus said he has given us his authority to overcome the spiritual attacks against us (Luke 10:18–19). I prayed. John, as my husband, my head, prayed as well. We commanded this foul spirit to leave me by the authority given to believers in Jesus Christ. Deliverance came. Victory. Release. Healing. Restoration. It was the final key. I needed to address all three aspects—my body, soul, and spirit—in order to come more fully into healing. Far too many women will focus only on one or two aspects and not engage in the spiritual warfare that is swirling around us.

But if we would be free, we must.

RELATIONAL ATTACKS

Another common enemy that often is at work in women's relationships is a spirit of accusation. In our friendships, in our relationships with peers at work, and especially in our marriages, we often feel that we are a disappointment to others, that they disapprove of us. We feel in their presence that we are not enough, or that we are too much. After we leave a time with them, we're plagued by a deep sense of failing. We feel frustrated and irritated and ashamed that we feel that way. Our hearts often land in shame and isolation, or we go to resentment . . . and isolation.

Do you know what I am talking about? Do you recognize this in your own life? That replaying of conversations you've had with people, that sense of having blown it, or that other sense of just being really irritated at them? Have you noticed how the feelings grow as you continue to mull it over? Now, who do you suppose would have a vested interest in ruining your relationships? This is exactly what Paul warned the Corinthians about when he said, "For we are not unaware of his schemes" (2 Cor. 2:11).

Well, a spirit of accusation was operating in *our* marriage for the first ten years of our married life. I felt John's disapproval over how I spent my time, my relationship with God, even how I chopped vegetables. I felt as though everything I did disappointed him somehow. I could not live up to his (unspoken) desires. It's hard to offer your heart and love to a person when you feel that way. Our tendency is to withdraw in shame or anger. At least, that's what I do.

Then one night, after an unusually uncomfortable dinner, John wanted to know how he was failing me. He often felt, he said, that I was disappointed in *him*, that he couldn't do anything right, that I disapproved of how he lived and who he was.

What?!

This was unbelievable to me. I felt nothing of the sort toward him. I wanted to be more like him. I told him that I didn't feel that way toward him, but I certainly felt that *from* him—felt that I was a deep disappointment *to him*. He told me that was utterly untrue. He felt nothing of the sort. It was then that John and I realized we were not alone in the room. We were being attacked by a spirit of accusation that had effectively worked between us for ten years, operating to isolate us from one another and ultimately destroy our marriage.

We got mad. Together, we took a stand against it and commanded it to leave. This can feel a little weird at first, talking to the air and saying stuff like, "I bring the cross of Christ against you. In Jesus' name I command you to leave." Sometimes you have to be firm and pray several times. As Peter said, "*firm* in the faith" (1 Peter 5:9, emphasis added). But leave it does!

What a relief. What a breakthrough for us. To be able to look into my husband's eyes now and not have mine clouded over by false accusation allowed me to see his love for me as true and real and deep. We now could believe that we liked each other, were *for* each other, and that the truest thing in our marriage was committed love.

It changed everything.

A WARRING BRIDE

Ladies, you are the Bride of Christ . . . and the Bride of Christ is a warring bride.

Now, often the hardest person to fight for is . . . yourself. But you must. Your heart is *needed.* You must be present and engaged in order to love well and fight on behalf of others. Without you, much will be lost. It is time to take a stand and to stand firm. We are at war. You are needed.

Yes, men are created in the image of the Warrior King. Men are warriors. But women need to fight too. It is a powerful good when a man battles for a woman's heart and stands between her and her enemies. But often, there is not a man present in a woman's life to fight on her behalf. And even when there is, God desires the woman's spirit to rise up in his strength as well. One day we will be queens—we will rule with Jesus (Rev. 21). We need to grow in our understanding and practice of spiritual warfare not only because we are being attacked but because it is one of the primary ways that we grow in Christ. He uses spiritual warfare in our lives to strengthen our faith, to draw us closer to him, to train us for the roles we are meant to play, to encourage us to play those roles, and to prepare us for our future at his side.

It is *not* that we are abandoned. Christ has not abandoned us. It is *not* that we are alone. He will never leave us or forsake us. It is *not* even up to us. The battle is the Lord's.

Jesus came through for us before we were even born. He fought for us before we even knew we needed him. He came; he died; he rose again *for us*. He was given all authority in heaven and on earth *for us* (Eph. 1:22). He has won the decisive victory against our Enemy. *But we must apply it*. Christianity is not a passive religion. It is an invasion of a Kingdom. We who are on the Lord's side must wield his victory. We must learn to enforce it. Women need to grow as warriors because we, too, were created to reign. God said of Eve as well as Adam, "and let them rule" (Gen. 1:26). And one day we will rule again (Matt. 25:21; Rev. 22:5). God allows spiritual warfare and uses it in our lives for our good. It is how we learn to grow in exercising our God-given spiritual authority as women.

There is a fascinating verse in Judges 2. Talking about how hard it was to gain the Promised Land, it explains that the Lord, the God of angel armies, did not drive all the nations out at once "by giving them into the hands of Joshua" (2:23). No, the Lord left some nations to test the Israelites who had not experienced war and to "teach warfare to the descendants of the Israelites who had not had previous battle experience" (3:2). Much of what he allows in your life is not for you to simply accept, *but to get you to rise up!* God wants you to know how to wield the weapons of warfare, how to take a stand, and how to fight.

> *"One day you will be a Queen and you must open your eyes."*
> —WILLIAM WALLACE TO THE PRINCESS IN *BRAVEHEART*

Women are not meant to be helpless creatures. God has given us a fierceness that is holy and is to be used on behalf of others. Chapters 4 and 5 in the book of Judges tells the story of Deborah, a prophetess who led Israel. Through her, God commanded the Israelites to go to war against Sisera and the Canaanite armies. The leader of the Israelite army, a man named Barak, would go to war only if Deborah went with them. He would not go if she did not. So Deborah went. "But because of the way you are going about this," said Deborah, "the honor will not be yours, for the LORD will hand Sisera over to a woman" (Judg. 4:9).

The story of the battle is short. Led by Deborah, the Israelites were victorious. Their enemy Sisera, however, escaped and fled on foot to the tent of Jael, a wife and the "most blessed of [the] tent-dwelling women" (5:24). While Israel's enemy slept in her tent, Jael took a tent peg and hammered it through his temple. He lay dead at her feet. Now, that is a fierce woman! And Deborah led Israel in a victory song:

> So may all your enemies perish, O LORD! But may they who love
> you be like the sun when it rises in its strength. (Judges 5:31)

WARRIOR PRINCESSES

What does a warrior princess look like? Think Joan of Arc. Think Mother Teresa. Think Esther. Think Mary of Bethany. Think Arwen. Think Éowyn. Think Deborah. Think Mary, Jesus' mother. Women who were wise, cunning, strong, beautiful, courageous, victorious, and very *present*.

I just returned home from a women's retreat where God came for his women. It was stunningly beautiful. My friend Susie was there, and she told me the following story about how Jesus came for her and two of her roommates in one fell swoop and taught them to take their stand against the enemy.

The evening session was on "Healing the Wound," and the women had been released into an hour-long covenant of silence so they could listen to God. They were asking God to reveal the lies they had been living under, the sentences they had agreed with, and the vows they had made as a result. We had prayed God's grace and courage for them that they would renounce the lies, however true they felt, and invite God in to heal their wounded hearts and speak the truth. Women were journaling, praying, weeping, seeking God, and inviting him into the deep places of their hearts to reveal and to heal.

Susie went back to her room to journal, as did two of her roommates. The number one lie of the enemy she realized she had believed and lived with all her life was, "Do not speak. Do not speak. Do not speak." Unbeknownst to her, roommate number one was journaling the key lie she had been living under: "You have nothing of value to offer. Do not offer. Do not offer. Do not offer." Roommate number two was writing down the lie she had lived with and believed: "No one will be there for you. You are too much trouble anyway. Do not ask. Do not ask. Do not ask."

It was then that "Do not ask" began to have a major asthma attack, and "Do not ask" does not have asthma. Has never had asthma. Susie's children do have severe asthma; she has been to the emergency room countless times with them. At once she recognized the attack for what it was. But Susie was in a covenant of silence. She was not supposed to talk. Her lie was screaming at her, "Do not speak!" yet she risked asking the choking, gasping woman, "Are you all right?" The struggling-to-breathe woman shooed Susie off with an "I'm fine," all the while hearing, "Do not ask! Do not ask! Do not ask!"

"Do not offer" was watching and listening and sensing that her roommate was in trouble, but she was frozen, believing she had nothing to offer. She was hearing, "Do not offer; do *not* offer; do *NOT* offer!" The three of them continued this for life-threatening minutes. "Do not speak," "Do not offer," and "Do not ask," a triangle of death until Susie saw that her roommate was turning blue, desperately gasping for breath and in dire need. Susie grabbed "Do not offer" and said, "I need your help!" They both went over to "Do not ask" and began to pray for God's help. Susie spoke loudly in the name of Jesus and commanded this assault on her roommate to cease. "Do not offer" lent her strength, joining in Susie's prayer, and immediately "Do not ask" was freed and breathing deeply. She was saved. Rescued. It was not asthma. It was spiritual attack.

The three women stood in wonder and began to share what their key lies were. They were astounded as they realized that God had come for them and unseated their lies, exposing them for what they were in one dramatic intervention. "Do not speak" needed to speak. "Do not offer" needed to offer. "Do not ask" was in need and was worth fighting for. The three of them became joyous—giddy even—and laughed together until their sides ached as they realized the wild love of Jesus. He had taken them out of the lecture and into the lab, showing them the destructive power of the lies they were living under and calling them to truth and to life.

Women warriors are strong, yes, and they are also tender. There is mercy in them. There is vulnerability. In fact, offering a tender vulnerability can only be done by an incredibly strong woman, a woman rooted in Christ Jesus who knows *whose* she is and therefore knows *who* she is. Offering our hearts wisely, living in the freedom of God's love, inviting others to rest, alluring those in our lives to the heart of God, and responding to the heart of God in worship are some of the most powerful ways that a woman wars for her world. But she also puts on the full armor of God *daily* and takes her immovable stand against the powers of darkness.

Satan is defeated. The prince of this world is cast down (John 12:30–32). The rulers and authorities are disarmed (Col. 2:15). But the demonic realm is a realm of lies, hatred, and murder. Satan and the fallen angels, now demons, have been cast down, but they are not chained. Not yet. Now, "Your enemy the devil prowls around like a roaring lion looking for someone to devour" (1 Peter 5:8). And he does devour. He assaults and maims and steals and kills and destroys wherever he can, and the brunt of his malice falls on God's image bearers. On you and me. On the Beloved. Satan is a vicious, ruthless bully, and a bully will not back down unless someone stronger stands up to him and exposes him for what he is. That is your job for "greater is He who is in you than he who is in the world" (1 John 4:4 NASB).

> Finally, be strong in the Lord and in his mighty power. Put on the full armor of God so that you can take your stand against the devil's schemes. For our struggle is not against flesh and blood, but against the rulers, against the authorities, against the powers of this dark world and against the spiritual forces of evil in the heavenly realms. Therefore put on the full armor of God, so that when the day of evil comes, you may be able to stand your ground, and after you have done everything, to stand. (Eph. 6:10–13)

There is a Daily Prayer that John and I and our ministry team pray every morning. It is good and true and enormously helpful. You'll find it at the back of this book. It is also gender neutral. A dear friend told us once that while she was praying on the armor of God, she saw it in her spirit's eye, and it was light and lovely. God made you a woman. On purpose. Perhaps it would help you to know that in wearing the armor of God, nothing is diminished—not your beauty, your femininity, or your tender, merciful, mighty heart.

A lovely young woman wrote me and told me that as she takes great care in dressing in the morning, so she takes great care in putting on the armor of God. Listen to the first part of her prayer.

> I now put on with thanks the armor which You have provided for me—girding myself with the belt of truth; binding up all that is vulnerable of my femininity; first my need to be pursued and fought for. Thank You for daily pursuing me and fighting for me as well.

I also gird up my desire to be irreplaceable in a grand scheme of Yours. You have placed this desire within me and I wrap Your truth around it, in hope of what You will do. Grant me eyes to see each day in light of Your activity, to live in the big-ness of Your story.

I gird up my desire to offer life through my gifting, the beauty You have bestowed on me. I ask You to continue to reveal and confirm what You desire to do through me and all You have given to me. I trust that You have called me by name and have given me a love, a beauty, a gift to pour out on my family, my friends, and those You bring to me. May this day be an offering of love poured out before You on the altar of my life.

Let us say it again. Your life is a Love Story set in the midst of a life-and-death battle. The beauty, the adventure, the intimacy— they are what are *most* real. But it is a battle to gain them and a battle to keep them. A battle for your own heart and a battle for the hearts around you. "The LORD is a warrior; the LORD is his name" (Ex. 15:3). Jesus fights on your behalf and on behalf of those you love. He asks you to join him.

CHAPTER TWELVE

An Irreplaceable Role

❦

*If there is a real woman—even the trace of one—still there inside the
grumbling, it can be brought to life again. If there's one wee spark
under all those ashes, we'll blow it till the whole pile is red and clear.*
—C. S. Lewis

*Mary responded, "I am the Lord's servant, and I am willing to accept
whatever he wants. May everything you have said come true."*
—Luke 1:38 nlt

The story of Cinderella turns upon an invitation.

Up until the moment that the courier from the palace arrives
at her door, Cinderella's life seems set in stone. She will always be
a washerwoman, a cellar girl. Her enemies will forever have the
upper hand. She will live a life of enduring disappointments,
though she will suffer them nobly. No other life seems possible.
This is her fate. Then, word from the prince arrives—an invitation to a ball. It is at this point that all hell breaks loose. Her longings are awakened. Her enemies become enraged. And her life is
never the same.

How gracious that it comes by invitation. As a woman, you
don't need to strive or arrange; you don't need to make it happen.
You only need to respond. Granted—Cinderella's response took

immense courage, courage that came only out of a deep desire to find the life her heart knew it was meant for. She *wanted* to go. But it took steadfastness to press through her fears just to get to the ball. It took courage not to abandon all hope even *after* she danced with the prince. (She ran back to the cellar, as we all do.) But she became the woman she was born to be, and the kingdom was never the same. It is a beautiful parable.

The same holds true for Mary, the mother of Jesus—only it's far, far more weighty. Her life also turned upon an invitation. The angel came as the courier of the King. But still, she needed to say yes. He would not force the whole thing upon her. Her heart needed to be willing. She would *need* her heart through all that followed. Accepting God's invitation required remarkable courage, and once again all hell broke loose. Her Enemy raged. She nearly lost her marriage. She and Joseph certainly lost their standing in the synagogue. Her life became an incredible story. Mary needed a steadfastness of heart to keep saying yes to God. But she became the woman she was born to be, and the Kingdom was never the same. It all started with an *invitation*.

The invitations of our Prince come to us in all sorts of ways. Your heart itself, as a woman, is an invitation. An invitation delivered in the most intimate and personalized way. Your Lover has written something on your heart. It is a call to find a life of Romance and to protect that love affair as your most precious treasure. A call to cultivate the beauty you hold inside, and to unveil your beauty on behalf of others. And it is a call to adventure, to become the *ezer* the world desperately needs you to be.

THE POWER OF A WOMAN'S LIFE

When the history of the world is finally told rightly—one of the great joys when we reach the Wedding Feast of the Lamb—it will be as clear as day that women have been essential to every great move of God upon this earth.

I wanted to say "*nearly* every great move," not wanting to overstate a crucial point and recognizing that there are moments when men have led the way. But Stasi chimed in and said, "Those men had mothers, didn't they?!" I was thinking of Moses who seemed to lead the Exodus, but it quickly dawned on me that it was his mother who saved his life as a baby (at the risk of her own life and the lives of her entire family). It was his sister who stayed with the babe and suggested a nursemaid when pharaoh's daughter took him for her own. (That nurse would be, of course, his mother.) Okay. I concede. Women have been essential to every great movement of God.

Certainly there are those amazing moments in the Old Testament like the story of Rahab, who secured the Hebrews' successful military launch into the Promised Land. And Esther, who saved her people from genocide and secured the future of Israel . . . and of the world. It's clear that women supported the ministry of Jesus, financially and emotionally, and women were the ones who stayed with him when nearly all the men hightailed it and ran. As we read the story of the spreading gospel and the birth of the church in the New Testament, we encounter women like Lydia, whose home became the staging point for the evangelism of Thyatira and Philippi; women like Nympha and Apphia, who hosted the emerging church in their homes—again, at great risk to themselves and their loved ones. There is Priscilla, who risked her life to help Paul spread the gospel, and Junias, who was with Paul when he was in prison and whom he called "outstanding among the apostles" (Rom. 16:7).

And of course, the salvation of mankind rested on the courage of a woman, a teenage girl. What if she had said no? What if any of them had said no?

To try and give honor to women in the sweep of history is

impossible here. It would be easier to think of any of the great or small turning points in God's rescue of mankind and try to find one where women were *not* irreplaceable. From the beginning, Eve was God's gift to the world—his *ezer kenegdo* for us. History is still unfolding, and your existence on this earth as a woman is proof that you have an irreplaceable role to play. You are a woman, are you not? An *ezer kenegdo* to your core. Your lingering disbelief (may it be fading away) that anything important hangs on your life is only evidence of the long assault on your heart by the one who knows who you could be and fears you.

There is much life saving that needs to be done yet, and someone needs to do it. Not in a pressure-filled, *You'd better get to it* kind of a way. Rather, an invitation. Your feminine heart is an invitation by your Creator. To what? To play an irreplaceable role in his Story. Isn't that what your Lover wrote there? Some dream, some desire, something so core to who you are it almost hurts to think of it. The very longing is such a part of your being it's scary even to give it a voice. You may not know the dream itself yet. But you know the *longing* to play an irreplaceable part. That is a good beginning.

Ezer is woven into the fabric of your feminine heart. You must live this out. What lives, what destinies are hanging on *your* yes to God?

YOUR IRREPLACEABLE ROLE

Our friend Jeanine has been a career missionary with OMS for thirty-two years. For the last fourteen, she has been pouring out her life in Medellín, Colombia—a city and a country infamous for drug cartels, murders, violence—a culture of death. It is not a place friendly to Christianity. "Sixty pastors a year are murdered in Colombia," she told us on a recent visit. Jeanine first followed God's call to teach Hebrew in a seminary there. Then he upped the stakes, asking her to minister in the country's notorious prisons. A single woman, walking into overcrowded, all-male prisons filled with hardened criminals—an incarnation of hell on earth—to bring the love of Jesus.

In Bellavista, a Colombian prison in Medellín, more than 6,000 inmates are crammed into a prison designed to hold 1,500. "Up until (14) years ago when the Bible studies began, Bellavista was known for its violence—there was an average of two murders *a day* within the prison walls . . . As lives are being transformed, the killings are slowing," she said. Only seven inmates were murdered from 1990 to 1997. Jeanine risks death daily, but she does not keep that from stopping her. For as she says, "Security is not found in the absence of danger, but in the presence of Jesus." More than five hundred inmates are currently studying Scripture at the prison, and literally thousands have been saved through the ministry Jeanine started. She is their *ezer*. The *ezer* to many in Colombia.

Our dear friend Carol has a bright mind and a keen intellect. A favorite among her professors, she graduated from an Ivy League university at the top of her class. Her mother is a professional, her father a university professor, her sister a physician, and her brother is finishing a law degree. The sky is the limit for Carol. She reads constantly. She is aware of international events and analyzes world trends. She plans her days so as not to miss National Public Radio broadcasts. And she just gave up what looked like a golden career move to stay at home full time with her newborn son.

There is nothing on earth Carol would rather do—yet it was an incredibly difficult decision to make. Her family doesn't understand; she feels she has let them down. She has hopes and desires to pursue a higher education. There is much that she wants to do, to learn, to experience. She has given up so much of her own life in order to bring life to her little boy. Learning to mother her child is requiring more of her heart and soul than she thought possible. God called Carol to the high position of mothering, and she is choosing to die a thousand small deaths to her self every single day while at the same time falling ever more in love with her son.

Carol chose to say yes to God and followed his lead into the hidden life of a stay-at-home mom. God is meeting her there. In the hiddenness, she is discovering the holy. And she is playing the most irreplaceable, essential, powerful, life-impacting role imaginable. As G. K. Chesterton wrote,

> To be Queen Elizabeth within a definite area, deciding sales, banquets, labors, and holidays; to be Whitely within a certain area, providing toys, boots, cakes, and books; to be Aristotle within a certain area, teaching morals, manners, theology, and hygiene; I can understand how this might exhaust the mind, but I cannot imagine how it could narrow it. How can it be a large career to tell other people's children about the Rule of Three, and a small career to tell one's own children about the universe? How can it be broad to be the same thing to everyone and narrow to be everything to someone? No, a woman's function is laborious, but because it is gigantic, not because it is minute. (*What's Wrong with the World*)

On Ellie Claus's seventeenth birthday, she crossed the finish line as the Junior Iditarod Champion—a 150-mile dogsled race through the Alaskan wilderness. Ellie lives in "the bush," the outback of Alaska, where she has grown up with the untamed wilderness as her backyard. It has been her dream to compete in the full-fledged Iditarod Trail Sled Dog Race, a 1,150-mile cross-country trek from Anchorage to Nome. (You have to be eighteen to run the Iditarod.) Polar bears prowl part of the route. Wolves too. Mushers are sometimes attacked by moose. Temperatures can dip to seventy degrees below zero. Competitors run the nine- to twelve-day race alone, without any outside assistance, on just a couple of hours' sleep a day.

Ellie is a petite, darling young woman you'd picture more at home at a prep school or on a dance team than running the dangerous Iditarod. But Ellie's heart is alive and passionate, thanks to her love of God. She is willing to take enormous risks to become the woman that she is meant to be. In 2004, twelve days after she turned eighteen, Ellie became the youngest person (man or woman) to run the Iditarod. She crossed the finish line after eleven days, nineteen hours, and twenty-four minutes, finishing forty-fifth out of a field of eighty-seven. Her grandmother runs marathons (twenty to date) and her mom guides backcountry skiing in Alaska. Women of adventure, each of them!

My friend Tammy has been a leader in women's ministry for decades. She is a gifted woman, totally sold out to God. And a few years ago God invited her to come away with him and sit at his feet. Alone. He called her to leave her position on the church staff. He called her to quit leading her small group, her Bible study, her accountability group. He asked her to become a woman of "one thing"—to become a Mary, a woman devoted to worship. To minister to the heart of God.

Tammy chose to say yes to God and followed his lead into the secret realm of his heart. Her friends thought she was nuts. The church leaders chastised her publicly for abandoning the Great Commission. She was accused and misunderstood. It hurt. But God had captured Tammy's heart and has been capturing it ever more deeply since. She has been captivated by his beauty. And his radiant beauty shines forth from her countenance.

Tammy became a worshiper, and her life of pouring her adoring devotion onto Jesus has become a beacon and a call to countless women to do the same—to attain to the high and holy calling of ministering to the heart of God and to discover ever more the treasure of who he is. I am one of those women who have been changed by her life. Tammy is playing her amazing, irreplaceable role very well.

Kathleen felt the call of God to become a doctor early in her life. As the daughter of an OB-GYN, she was exposed early and often to the cost paid by doctors and their families—the long hours, the sleepless nights, the inconvenient emergencies. Kathleen has also been captured by the call of Christ to third world countries. She is pursuing her medical degree overseas so that she can play her irreplaceable role as a missionary doctor, bringing physical healing through her expertise and spiritual healing through her God.

You see, our true places as women in God's Story are as diverse and unique as wildflowers in a field. No two look quite the same. But we all share certain spheres of influence to which we are called to be an *ezer*.

IN YOUR RELATIONSHIPS

Eve is God's relational specialist given to the world *to keep relationship a priority.*

Men have a way of letting these things slip. They'll go months without checking in on the health of their relationships. Years, even. And the World simply uses people, then spits them out when they are worn out and no longer "on top of their game." Our Enemy despises relationship, hates love in any form, fears its redemptive power. This is why God sent Eve. Women are *needed* to protect relationships, bring them back to center stage where they belong. You might at times feel like the only one who cares. But as women we must hang on to this—that because of the Trinity, relationship is *the* most important thing in the universe. Let us not give way or yield our intuitive sense of the importance of relationship for anything.

It is here, *starting* in our circles of intimacy, that we are first and foremost women. It is here that we must first turn our gaze to ask,

"What does it look like to offer my Beauty, my fierce devotion, my love? How do they need me to be their *ezer*?" You have an irreplaceable role in your relationships. No one can be to the people in your life who you can be to them. No one can offer what you can offer. There are many things God calls us to do, but loving well always comes first. And don't your relationships feel *opposed*? Of course. They must be fought for.

Satan knew that to take out Adam, all he had to do was take out Eve—his *ezer kenegdo*. It worked rather well, and he has not abandoned the basic plan ever since. Your place in the world as God's heart for relationship is vital. All the Enemy has to do to destroy people's lives is to get them isolated, a lamb separated from the flock. To do this he removes the *ezers* in their life. He makes a woman feel like, *What do I have to offer, really? They're probably doing fine.* Don't you believe it for a moment. You have been sent by the Trinity on behalf of love, of relationships. Fight for them.

In the Body of Christ

Your life is also part of a larger movement, a mystical fellowship, the Kingdom of God advancing here on earth. That fellowship of the Ransomed being Restored—that is an amazing fellowship to be a part of. To be sure, it's messy. Have you noticed in Paul's letters to the young church how often he has to intervene in relationships? "I plead with Euodia and I plead with Syntyche to agree with each other in the Lord" (Phil. 4:2). He's addressing two women there, by the way. The fellowship of Christ is *messy* because it, too, is *opposed*. And here you have an irreplaceable role to play.

Yes, we know—women haven't always felt welcomed to bring their gifts to their churches, unless those gifts fall within certain narrow parameters (the nursery, the bake sale, etc.). We haven't time here to address the issues surrounding "the proper role of women" in the church. That would also take a book in itself. However, we do believe it is far more helpful to start with *Design*—with what God designed a woman to be and to offer. That comes first. Understand Design and you can then interpret roles. A woman is *not* the same as a man (thank God!). She is designed differently. We hope that's clear by now. Doesn't it follow that her contributions will be uniquely feminine? And therefore the roles she plays will best fit her feminine heart? (Not as Fallen Eve, but as Redeemed and Restored Eve.)

Furthermore, many of the Scriptures on the *Role* of women in the church are a reflection of God's concern for a woman's protection and spiritual covering. We live in a dangerous world. Satan's opposition of the Church is vicious. He bears a special hatred for Eve. It follows that God would want to ensure that a woman helping to advance his Kingdom would be offered the covering and protection of good men. Issues of headship and authority are intended for the *benefit* of women, not their suppression. You know how dangerous it can be to try and come alive as a truly feminine woman. Right?

God desires that wherever and however you offer yourself to the Body of Christ, you'll have the protection of good men over you. Not to hold you back, but to set you free as a woman. Christ has made man as his warrior, to offer his strength on behalf of Eve *so that she might flourish*. If that's not the context you've found yourself in, find one that is. After all, when we speak of your irreplaceable role within the Body of Christ, we're talking about the true fellowship of those whose hearts are captured for Jesus, who have become his intimate allies. You want to offer yourself to those who thirst for what you have. If it's not wanted where you are, ask Jesus what he wants you to do.

If you are called, God will make a way. Either where you are or through a change of circumstances. Follow your Lover; respond to his invitations. With him, there is no stopping you.

In the World

Stepping further out into your farthest sphere of influence, you have something essential to offer the World. It may be in the form of a notable career. It may be a hidden life, well lived. Some women are called to the marketplace. Lydia was an entrepreneur when Paul met her, "a dealer in purple cloth from the city of Thyatira, who was a worshiper of God" (Acts 16:14). Deborah was an advisor to Israel on matters of justice, economics, and warfare (Judg. 4–5). Some women find themselves in the marketplace of the World because they want to be there. It is their calling. Others are there because at this time in their lives they have no choice.

Either way, the crucial issue is this: it is *as a woman* you must live there. Do not be naive. The World is still deeply marred by the Fall. Men still dominate in many sinful ways (remember the curse). Women who "make it" there tend to be dominating and controlling (remember Fallen Eve). The Evil One holds sway over the World and its systems (1 John 5:19). In the World you *must* be as cunning as a Rahab, an Esther, a Tamar. You must walk wisely. You must not let them shape you into their view of what a woman is. You'll end up a man. What you have to offer is *as a woman*. Uniquely feminine.

Above all, you must live in that World as a response to the invitation of Jesus, for you will be hurt if he has not called you there. You will be covered if he has.

What Is Written on Your Heart?

As I said earlier, the invitations of Jesus come to us in many ways. Sometimes they come through a circumstance, an opportunity that opens before us. Sometimes they come through other people who see something in us that we may not yet see, and they invite us to step forth in some way. But God's invitations ultimately are matters of the heart. They come through our passions, those desires set deep within us. What is it you yearn to see happen—how do *you* long for the world to be a better place? What makes you so angry you nearly see red? What brings you to tears?

You will find that as God restores your heart and sets you free, you will recover long-lost passions, long-forsaken dreams. You'll find yourself drawn to some vision for making the world a better place. Those emerging desires are invitations—not to rush out and attempt them immediately. That also is naive. They are invitations to bring your heart to your Lover and ask him to clarify, to deepen, to speak to you about how and when and with whom. We love Frederick Buechner's description when he writes, "The place that God calls us is that place where the world's deep hunger and our deep desire meet."

Do Not Give Way to Fear

Of course this is scary.

Responding to the invitations of Jesus often feels like the riskiest thing we've ever done. Just ask Rahab, Esther, Ruth, and Mary. Ask Jeanine, Ellie, Tammy, Carol, and Kathleen. Webster defines *risk* as exposing one's life to the possibility of injury, damage, or loss. The life of the friends of God is a life of profound risk. The risk of loving others. The risk of stepping out and offering, speaking up and following our God-given dreams. The risk of playing the irreplaceable role that is ours to play. Of course it is hard. If it were easy, you'd see lots of women living this way.

So let's come back then to what Peter said when he urged women to offer their beauty to others in love. This is the secret of femininity unleashed:

Do not give way to fear. (1 Peter 3:6)

The reason we fear to step out is because we know that it might not go well (is that an understatement?). We have a history of wounds screaming at us to play it safe. We feel so deeply that if it doesn't go well, if we are not received well, their reaction becomes the verdict on our lives, on our very beings, on our hearts. We fear that our deepest doubts about ourselves as women will be confirmed. Again. That we will hear yet again the message of our wounds, the piercing negative answers to our Question. That is why we can *only* risk stepping out when we are resting in the love of God. When we have received his verdict on our lives—that we are chosen and dearly loved. That he finds us captivating. Then we are free to offer.

You could say that people did not respond very well to Jesus' love, to his stepping out in faith and playing the role that was his alone to play. And that would be a ridiculous understatement. The very people that Jesus died for hurled insults at him, mocked him, spat at him, crucified him. Jesus had to trust his Father *profoundly*, with his very being. Peter uses him as our example saying, "Follow in his steps . . . He did not retaliate when he was insulted. When he suffered, he did not threaten to get even. He left his case in the hands of God" (1 Peter 2:21–23 NLT). Or, as another translation has it, "he entrusted himself" to God. He was okay. He entrusted himself to God.

A few verses later Peter, writing to women, says, "In the same way . . . do not give way to fear" (3:1, 6). Jesus lived a life of love, and he invites us to do the same. Regardless of the response.

It was very hard and immensely risky for me to begin to speak and offer from my heart at our women's retreats. Terrifying, really. You see, when I first began to speak, I was severely overweight and struggle here still. My sin, my addiction, was plain for all to see. To stand in front of a group of women and be clearly failing in the outward beauty department was humbling and hard. It has felt risky for me to write this book with John. Risky to share so much of my story. Risky because I'm a first-time author and he is so well-known, so good at it.

But we don't get to wait to offer our lives until we have our acts together. We don't get that luxury. If we did, would anyone *ever* feel like offering *anything*? God asks us to be vulnerable. He invites us to share and give in our weaknesses. He wants us to offer the beauty that he has given us even when we are keenly aware that it is not all that we wish it were. He wants us to *trust* him.

How it turns out is no longer the point. Living in this way, as a woman alive, is a choice we make because it is the woman we want to be. It is our loving response to our Lover's invitation.

BE PRESENT

John and I were at a newcomers' dessert-type thing, a get-acquainted deal where, as part of our introductions to each other, we were to share what our family motto was. In our little group was an older couple we had been drawn to. The gentleman had a twinkle in his eye, a spark, as if he had discovered the secret to life and it brought him much joy. His wife was a tiny woman who I can best describe as being very *present*. She was not a woman hiding, nor a woman afraid. She was a woman at rest, at home with herself and with all pistons firing. She was alive and beautiful.

The gentleman looked to his wife and asked, "Do we have a family motto?" She answered, "Well, it's been on the refrigerator for the past thirty years." He asked, "What? Amana?" After some laughter, this is what she shared. This is what she lived by. This is what she invited others into.

> Now we should live when the pulse of life is strong. Life is a tenuous thing . . . fragile, fleeting. Don't wait for tomorrow. Be here now! Be here now! Be here now!

Be here now.

To live as an authentic, ransomed, and redeemed woman means to be real and present in this moment. If we continue to hide, much will be lost. We cannot have intimacy with God or anyone else if we stay hidden and offer only who we think we ought to be or what we believe is wanted. We cannot play the *ezer* role we were meant to play if we remain bound by shame and fear, presenting only to the world the face we have learned is safe. *You have only one life to live. It would be best to live your own.*

What have we to offer, really, other than who we are and what God has been pouring into our lives? It was not by accident that you were born; it was not by chance that you have the desires you do. The Victorious Trinity has planned on your being here now, "for such a time as this" (Est. 4:14). We need you.

> Jesus knew that the Father had put all things under his power, *and that he had come from God and was returning to God*; so he got up from the meal, took off his outer clothing, and wrapped a towel around his waist. After that, he poured water into a basin and began to wash his disciples' feet, drying them with the towel that was wrapped around him. (John 13:3–5, emphasis added)

Jesus knew who he was. He knew where he had come from and where he was going. He knew why he was here. And so, in power and strength, in humility and complete freedom, he offers. He ministers to us and ultimately he pours out his life as an offering for ours. Pleasing and holy and acceptable. Jesus does this, he says, as "an example that you should do as I have done for you" (v. 15).

God really does want you to know who *you* are. He wants you to be able to understand the story of your life, to know where you have come from, and to know where you are going. There is freedom there. Freedom to be and to offer and to love. So, may we take a moment and remind you who you truly are?

You are a woman. An image bearer of God. The Crown of Creation. You were chosen before time and space, and you are wholly and dearly loved. You are sought after, pursued, romanced, the passionate desire of your Fiancé, Jesus. You are dangerous in your beauty and your life-giving power. And you are needed.

As a woman who has been ransomed and redeemed, you can be strong and tender. You speak to the world of God's mercy, mystery, beauty, and his desire for intimate relationship. You are inviting; you can risk being vulnerable, offering the weight of your life as well as your need for more because you are safe in God's love. You labor with God to bring forth life—in creativity, in work, in others. Your aching, awakened heart leads you to the feet of Jesus, where you wait on him and wait for him. The eyes of his heart are ever upon you. The King is captivated by your beauty.

We need you. We need you to awaken to God more fully and to awaken to the desires of the heart that he placed within you so that you will come alive to him and to the role that is yours to play. Perhaps you are meant to be a concert musician or a teacher. Perhaps you are meant to be a neurologist or a horse trainer. Perhaps you are to be an activist for ecology or the poor or the aged or the ill. You are certainly called to be a woman, wherever else he leads you.

And that is crucial, dear heart. Whatever your particular calling, you are meant to grace the world with your dance, to follow the lead of Jesus wherever he leads you. He will lead you first into himself; and then, with him, he will lead you into the world that he loves and needs you to love.

It is by Invitation.

TAKE MY HAND

There is a scene near the end of the film *Anna and the King* I wish I could now play for you. Let me describe it.

Captivating

The setting is nineteenth-century Siam, a tiny but beautiful Asian country still in the grips of its ancient past. Anna, an English woman living in Siam as a tutor to the king's many offspring, has helped King Mangkut prepare for a state dinner. He wants to show the British that his country is ready to enter into the affairs of the world, so the dinner is given in the English style—silverware, tablecloths, candlelight, and, at the end of the meal, ballroom dancing.

When the feast is over and it comes time for the first dance, the king stands and extends his hand to Anna. He invites her to dance with him. He fixes his gaze upon her and is distracted by nothing and no one else. He waits for her response. She is clearly surprised, taken aback, but has the grace to respond and stand. As they walk past the long table, the king's eyes never stray from hers, a smile playing on his lips. Others are upset that he has chosen her. Some watch with contempt, others with pleasure. It is of no consequence to the king or to Anna.

Anna came to the ball prepared. She was beautiful in a striking gown that shimmered like starlight. She spent hours getting herself ready—her hair, her dress, her heart. As they reach the dance floor, Anna expresses her fear of dancing with the king before the eyes of others. "We wouldn't want to end up in a heap," she says. His answer to her questioning heart? "I am King. I will lead."

Jesus is extending his hand to you. He is inviting you to dance with him. He asks, "May I have this dance . . . every day of your life?" His gaze is fixed on you. He is captivated by your beauty. He is smiling. He cares nothing of the opinion of others. He is standing. He will lead. He waits for your response.

My lover spoke and said to me,
"Arise, my darling,
my beautiful one, and come with me." (Song 2:10)

220

Epilogue

*T*he journey has begun.

The Romance has taken a fresh turn.

And the battle has been joined.

A few words of advice and encouragement before it all slips away. First, do *not* rush on to the next thing. The church is full of fads, the world a circus of distraction. You live in *The Matrix*; you live in a world at war. Do not put this book down while thinking to yourself, *That was nice. What's for dinner?* Your heart's journey is the central mission of your life; everything else depends on your success here. So stay with this! This way of life John and I have laid out here has utterly transformed the lives of thousands of women; they would tell you now there is nothing to compare with the freedom and life that can be had. But you must choose it. You must be intentional, or the world, your flesh, and the devil will have you for lunch.

Pray the Daily Prayer (in the appendix). It will rescue you. Some women have found it helpful to download the free audio version from our Web site (www.ransomedheart.com) and put it on their MP3 player or listen in the car while driving to work.

Ask some women friends to join you in a small group and go through *Captivating* together. Do the *Guided Journal* the second time around. It is like getting two years of counseling for about thirteen dollars. What a deal!

If you want to do a group—and you need other women in your life who want the same things you do, who want to pursue Jesus like you do—we have a *Captivating Heart to Heart* video series that will help you.

Our ministry offers a four-day Captivating conference that you might pray about attending. We also have CDs available from the live sessions at the retreats. Coming to a retreat or listening to it is a fantastic way to have the message go deeper within.

Now, if you are married, two things: Give your husband *Wild at Heart* to read (it's the masculine version of this book). The more he is restored as a man, the better for the both of you. Then, the two of you should read *Love and War*, which John and I wrote together about marriage from this point of view. It is *really* good. It also has a video series for couples and small groups to use!

Join the revolution. Go after other women. Teach a class; lead a small group; put on a retreat. We give you this message; use it to rescue others. It will be one of the most exciting things you ever do.

Pursue your further healing. Learn how to fight. Develop a conversational intimacy with God. Come to www.ransomedheart.com and dive into the community, resources, podcasts, and live events we offer. This is only the beginning. There is an entire kingdom waiting through this door.

SOME FINAL THOUGHTS . . .

Men need women. Men will not receive the healing and the transformation God desires to give them without the presence of women in their lives offering their wisdom, strength, grace, and mercy. Not only from their wives but also from their sisters, daughters, friends, and co-laborers in Christ. Godly femininity is magnificent and beautiful and necessary.

Women need men. We will always need them. We need them as a godly covering over us to protect us from other men, from the world, and especially from the enemy. Mary had Joseph. Esther had Mordecai. Ruth had Boaz. We will not become the women God intends us to be without the guidance, counsel, wisdom, strength, and love of good men in our lives. Men are fabulous. Hooray for men. Godly masculinity is a glorious and magnificent thing. No man bashing going on here.

We need each other. Remember, God gave the great mandate to "rule and subdue" the earth to both men and women *together*. The Kingdom of God is advancing "and the gates of Hell will not overcome it" (Matt. 16:18). But the Kingdom of God will not advance as it is meant to without half of the church doing her part. The feminine half. As Beth Moore says, "We don't want to take men's place. We want to take our own."

Every one of us has a call on our lives. Every single one of us. We all are needed in this grand Love Story that God is telling that is set in the midst of a terrible war. The call to join Aslan at the Round Table, to ride to Minis Tirith, to stand firm against the enemy, is a call to love. It is not about our glory but God's glory. It is not about reaping a great reward, though great rewards will be given. It is about LOVE.

Sisters, it all matters. The tiny little choices to love that are seen only by God matter as deeply as the grand ones. In fact, you can't make larger choices without them being built upon millions of smaller ones. Your choice to let the other car cut in front of you on the freeway, your choice to sponsor a child through a ministry like Compassion International or World Vision, your choice to volunteer in your child's classroom, or make a meal, or visit a home bound person, or pick up the neighbor's mail all matter more than any of us realize. Your choices to "serve one another in love" (Gal. 5:13) bring the Life of God to others and continue the transformation of your own soul.

> *"You must live the life you were born to live."*
> —THE REVEREND MOTHER, THE SOUND OF MUSIC

You are a princess. You are Daddy's cherished little girl and you always will be. You are the Beloved of God, chosen, holy, and dearly loved (Eph. 1:4). And you always will be! And you are, each and every one of you, an ambassador of Christ—reconciling the world to Jesus. "We are therefore Christ's ambassadors, as though God were making his appeal through us. We implore you on Christ's behalf: Be reconciled to God!" (2 Cor. 5:20).

The way our particular calling looks is as varied as the women reading this book. God has planted something in each one of our hearts. If you don't know what is planted in yours, ask yourself, "Where have I been wounded? What sentences have I been living under that have pinned my heart down and kept me from offering my unique beauty, from playing my irreplaceable role?" These are clues to your calling. Ask God. He will show you. None of us see quite as clearly as we long to yet. One day we will. In the meantime, ask Jesus.

Now, it will take courage. It will take risk. It will take faith. Loving always does.

"Perfect love drives out fear" (1 John 4:18).

It is Christmastime as I write. My world is shimmering with white lights and Christmas carols. We are remembering together once again the story that we were born into and the One who chose to be born into ours. The King of kings' arrival was heralded to shepherds, most likely cold and alone in the darkened fields.

Imagine it. The quiet night suddenly disturbed, dramatically, gloriously. An angel appears to them in the sky and then a host of angels telling them the good news. Telling them first to "Fear not!" Fear not. Johann Christoph Arnold said, "'Fear not' was more than an instruction for them to get off the ground and stop shielding their frightened faces. It was a declaration of war on fear."

God is telling us to lay aside our fear and trust him. Trust his love. Trust the goodness of his heart. And step out and risk in love.

There is a song written on your heart and you must sing it. The world is waiting, needing what it is you have to offer. You must live the life you were born to live.

A Prayer for Salvation

The most important relationship for every one of us is our relationship with Jesus Christ. Choosing to believe that he is who he claimed to be and receiving him by faith as your Lord and Savior is the most vital act anyone will ever do. We want life. He is Life. We need cleansing. He is the Living Water.

Here is a sample prayer if you have not yet given your life to Jesus and invited him into yours:

> *Jesus, I believe you are the Son of God, that you died on the cross to rescue me from sin and death and to restore me to the Father. I choose now to turn from my sins, my self-centeredness, and every part of my life that does not please you. I choose you. I receive your forgiveness and ask you to take your rightful place in my life as my Savior and Lord. Come reign in my heart, fill me with your love and your life, and help me to become a person who is truly loving—a person like you. Restore me, Jesus. Live in me; love through me. Thank you, God. In Jesus' name I pray. Amen.*

A Daily Prayer for Freedom

❧

*M*y dear Lord Jesus, I come to you now to be restored in you—to renew my place in you, my allegiance to you, and to receive from you all the grace and mercy I so desperately need this day. I honor you as my sovereign Lord, and I surrender every aspect of my life totally and completely to you. I give you my body as a living sacrifice; I give you my heart, soul, mind, and strength; and I give you my spirit as well. I cover myself with your blood—my spirit, my soul, and my body. And I ask your Holy Spirit to restore my union with you, seal me in you, and guide me in this time of prayer.

Dear God, holy and victorious Trinity, you alone are worthy of all my worship, my heart's devotion, all my praise and all my trust, and all the glory of my life. I worship you, bow to you, and give myself over to you in my heart's search for life. You alone are Life, and you have become my life. I renounce all other gods, all idols, and I give you the place in my heart and in my life that you truly deserve. I confess here and now that it is all about you, God, and not about me. You are the Hero of this story, and I belong to you. Forgive me for my every sin. Search me and know me and reveal to me any aspect of my life that is not pleasing to you, expose any agreements I have made with my Enemy, and grant me the grace of a deep and true repentance.

Heavenly Father, thank you for loving me and choosing me before you made the world. You are my true Father—my Creator, my Redeemer, my Sustainer, and the true end of all things, including my life. I love you; I trust you; I worship you. Thank you for proving your love for me by sending your only Son, Jesus, to be my sacrifice and my new life. I receive him and all his life and all his work, which you ordained for me. Thank you for including me in Christ, for forgiving me my sins, for granting me his righteousness, for making me complete in him. Thank you for making me alive with Christ, raising me with him, seating me with him at your right hand, granting me his authority, and anointing me with your Holy Spirit. I receive it all with thanks and give it total claim to my life.

Jesus, thank you for coming for me, for ransoming me with your own life. I honor you as my Lord; I love you, worship you, trust you. I sincerely receive you as my redemption, and I receive all the work and triumph of your crucifixion, whereby I am cleansed from all my sin through your shed blood, my old nature is removed, my heart is circumcised unto God, and every claim being made against me is disarmed. I take my place in your cross and death, whereby I have died with you to sin and to my flesh, to the world, and to the Evil One. I am crucified with Christ. I now take up my cross and crucify my flesh with all its pride, unbelief, and idolatry. I put off the old man. I now bring the cross of Christ between me and all people, all spirits, all things. Holy Spirit, apply to me the fullness of the work of the crucifixion of Jesus Christ for me. I receive it with thanks and give it total claim to my life.

Jesus, I also sincerely receive you as my new life, my holiness and sanctification, and I receive all the work and triumph of your resurrection, whereby I have been raised with you to a new life, to walk in newness of life, dead to sin and alive to God. I am crucified with Christ, and it is no longer I who live but Christ who lives in me. I now take my place in your resurrection, whereby I have been made alive with you, I reign in life through you. I put on the new person in all holiness and humility, in all righteousness and purity and truth. Christ is now my life, the one who strengthens me. Holy

Spirit, apply to me the fullness of the resurrection of Jesus Christ for me. I receive it with thanks and give it total claim to my life.

Jesus, I also sincerely receive you as my authority and rule, my everlasting victory over Satan and his kingdom, and I receive all the work and triumph of your ascension, whereby Satan has been judged and cast down, his rulers and authorities disarmed, all authority in heaven and on earth given to you, Jesus, and I have been given fullness in you, the Head over all. I take my place in your ascension, whereby I have been raised with you to the right hand of the Father and established with you in all authority.

I bring your authority and your Kingdom rule over my life, my family, my household, and my domain. And now I bring the fullness of your work—your cross, resurrection, and ascension—against Satan, against his kingdom, and against all his emissaries and all their work warring against me and my domain. Greater is he who is in me than he who is in the world. Christ has given me authority to overcome all the power of the Evil One, and I claim that authority now over and against every enemy, and I banish them in the name of Jesus Christ. Holy Spirit, apply to me the fullness of the work of the ascension of Jesus Christ for me. I receive it with thanks and give it total claim to my life.

Holy Spirit, I sincerely receive you as my Counselor, my Comforter, my Strength, and my Guide. Thank you for sealing me in Christ. I honor you as my Lord, and I ask you to lead me into all truth, to anoint me for all of my life and walk and calling, and to lead me deeper into Jesus today. I fully open my life to you in every dimension and aspect—my body, my soul, and my spirit—choosing to be filled with you, to walk in step with you in all things. Apply to me, blessed Holy Spirit, all of the work and all of the gifts in pentecost. Fill me afresh, blessed Holy Spirit. I receive you with thanks and give you total claim to my life.

Heavenly Father, thank you for granting to me every spiritual

blessing in the heavenlies in Christ Jesus. I receive those blessings into my life today, and I ask the Holy Spirit to bring all those blessings into my life this day. Thank you for the blood of Jesus. Wash me once more with his blood from every sin and stain and evil device. I put on your armor—the belt of truth, the breastplate of righteousness, the shoes of the readiness of the gospel of peace, the helmet of salvation. I take up the shield of faith and the sword of the Spirit, the Word of God, and I wield these weapons against the Evil One in the power of God. I choose to pray at all times in the Spirit, to be strong in you, Lord, and in your might.

Father, thank you for your angels. I summon them in the authority of Jesus Christ and release them to war for me and my household. May they guard me at all times this day. Thank you for those who pray for me; I confess I need their prayers, and I ask you to send forth your Spirit and rouse them, unite them, raising up the full canopy of prayer and intercession for me. I call forth the kingdom of the Lord Jesus Christ this day throughout my home, my family, my life, and my domain. I pray all of this in the name of Jesus Christ, with all glory and honor and thanks to him.

A Prayer for Sexual Healing

Healing for your sexuality is available; this is a very hopeful truth! But you must realize that your sexuality is very deep and core to your nature as a human being. Sexual brokenness can be one of the deepest types of brokenness a person experiences. You must take your healing and restoration seriously. This guided prayer will help immensely. You may find you need to pray through it a few times in order to experience a lasting freedom.

A bit of explanation on the reasons for the prayer: First, when we misuse our sexuality through sin, we give Satan an open door to oppress us in our sexuality. A man who uses pornography will find himself in a very deep struggle with lust; a woman who was sexually promiscuous before marriage may find herself wresting with sexual temptation years afterward. So it is important to bring our sexuality under the Lordship (and therefore protection) of the Lord Jesus Christ, and seek his cleansing of our sexual sins.

Second, sexual brokenness—whether through abuse of our sexuality by our own actions or by the actions of others—can create sexual difficulties, and also opens the door for the enemy to oppress us. Quite often forgiveness is needed—both the confidence that we are forgiven by the Lord and also the choice we make to forgive others. This will prove immensely freeing.

Let us begin by bringing our lives and sexuality under the Lordship of Jesus Christ:

231

Lord Jesus Christ, I confess here and now that you are my Creator (John 1:3) and therefore the creator of my sexuality. I confess that you are also my Savior, that you have ransomed me with your blood (1 Cor. 15:3; Matt. 20:28). I have been bought with the blood of Jesus Christ; my life and my body belong to God (1 Cor. 6:19–20). Jesus, I present myself to you now to be made whole and holy in every way, including in my sexuality. You ask us to present our bodies to you as living sacrifices (Rom. 12:1) and the parts of our bodies as instruments of righteousness (Rom. 6:13). I do this now. I present my body, my sexuality as a woman, and I present my sexual nature to you.

Next you need to renounce the ways you have misused your sexuality. The more specific you can be, the more helpful this will be. Your sexuality was created by God for pleasure and joy within the context of the marriage covenant. Sexual activity outside of marriage can be very damaging to a person and to relationships (1 Cor. 6:18–20). What you want to do in this part of the prayer is confess and renounce all sexual sin—for example, sexual intimacy outside of marriage. Not only intercourse, but other forms of sexual intimacy such as mutual masturbation or oral sex. Many people assume these "don't really count as sin" because they didn't result in actual intercourse; however, there was sexual stimulation and intimacy outside marriage. Keep in mind there is the "Spirit of the law" and the "letter of the law." What matters are issues of heart and mind as well as body. Other examples of sins to renounce would be marital affairs, the use of pornography, homosexual acts, and sexual fantasies.

You may know exactly what you need to confess and renounce; you may need to ask God's help to remember. Take your time here. As memories and events come to mind, confess and renounce them.

After you have confessed your sins—and don't get tied up trying to remember each and every one, just trust God to remind you—then go on with the rest of the prayer.

Jesus, I ask your Holy Spirit to help me now remember, confess, and renounce my sexual sins. [Pause. Listen. Remember. Confess and renounce.] *Lord Jesus, I ask your forgiveness for every act of sexual sin. You promised that if we confess our sins you are faithful and just to forgive us our sins and cleanse us from all unrighteousness (1 John 1:9). I ask you to cleanse me of my sexual sins now, cleanse my body, soul and spirit, cleanse my heart and mind and will, cleanse my sexuality. Thank you for forgiving me and cleansing me. I receive your forgiveness and cleansing. I renounce every claim I have given Satan to my life or sexuality through my sexual sins. Those claims are now broken by the Cross and blood of Jesus Christ (Col. 2:13–15).*

Next come issues of forgiveness. It is vital that you forgive both yourself and those who have harmed you sexually. LISTEN CAREFULLY: forgiveness is a *choice*; we often have to make the *decision* to forgive long before we *feel* forgiving. We realize this can be difficult, but the freedom you will find will be worth it! Forgiveness is not saying, "It didn't hurt me." Forgiveness is not saying, "It didn't matter." Forgiveness is the act whereby we pardon the person; we release them from all bitterness and judgment. We give them to God to deal with.

Lord Jesus, I thank you for offering me total and complete forgiveness. I receive that forgiveness now. I choose to forgive myself for all of my sexual wrongdoing. I also choose to forgive those who have harmed me sexually. [Be specific here; name those people, and forgive them.] *I release them to you. I release all my anger and judgment toward them. Come, Lord Jesus, into the pain they caused me and heal me with your love.*

This next step involves breaking the unhealthy emotional and spiritual bonds formed with other people through sexual sin. One of the reasons the Bible takes sexual sin so seriously is because of the damage it does. Another reason is because of the bonds it forms with people, bonds meant to be formed only between husband and wife (see 1 Cor. 6:15–20). One of the marvelous effects of the Cross of our Lord Jesus Christ is that it breaks these unhealthy bonds. "May I never boast except in the cross of our Lord Jesus Christ, through which the world has been crucified to me, and I to the world" (Gal. 6:14).

I now bring the Cross of my Lord Jesus Christ between me and every person with whom I have been sexually intimate. [Name them specifically whenever possible. Also, name those who have abused you sexually.] *I break all sexual, emotional, and spiritual bonds with* [name if possible, or just "that person in high school" if you can't remember the name]. *I keep the Cross of Christ between us.*

Many people experience negative consequences through the misuse of their sexuality. Those consequences might be lingering guilt (even after confession) or repeated sexual temptation. Consequences might also be the inability to enjoy sex with their spouse. It will help to bring the work of Christ here as well. Many people end up making unhealthy "agreements" about sex or themselves, about men or women or intimacy because of the damage they have experienced through sexual sin (their sin or the sin of someone against them). You will want to ask Christ what those agreements are and *break them*!

I renounce [name what the struggle is—"the inability to have an orgasm" or "this lingering shame" or "the hatred of my body"]. *I bring the Cross and blood of Jesus Christ against this* [guilt or shame, every negative consequence]. *Lord Jesus, I also ask you to reveal to me any agreements I have made about my sexuality or this specific struggle.* [An example would be "I will always struggle with this," or "I don't deserve to enjoy sex now," or "My sexuality is dirty." Pause and let Jesus reveal those agreements to you. Then break them.] *I break this agreement (name it) in the name of my Lord Jesus Christ, and I renounce every claim I have given it in my life.*

Finally, it will prove helpful to consecrate your sexuality to Jesus Christ once more.

Lord Jesus, I now consecrate my sexuality to you in every way. I consecrate my sexual intimacy with my spouse to you. I ask you to cleanse and heal my sexuality and our sexual intimacy in every way. I ask your healing grace to come and free me from all consequences of sexual sin. I ask you to fill my sexuality with your healing love and goodness. Restore my sexuality in wholeness. Let me and my spouse both experience all of the intimacy and pleasure you intended a man and woman to enjoy in marriage. I pray all of this in the name of Jesus Christ my Lord. Amen!!

We could report many, many stories of stunning redemption that have come as a result of individuals and couples praying through this type of prayer. Now remember—sometimes the wounds and consequences take time to heal. You might want to revisit this prayer several times over if lasting healing has not yet taken place.

You may recall actions that need confession long after you finish this book, so return to this prayer, and confess those as well. Some of you will also benefit from seeing a good Christian counselor. Hold fast to these truths:

You, your body, and your sexuality belong to Jesus Christ.

He has completely forgiven you.

He created your sexuality to be whole and holy.

He created your sexuality to be a source of intimacy and joy.

Jesus Christ came to seek and save "what was lost" (Luke 19:10), including all that was lost in the blessings he intended through our sexuality!

Acknowledgments

*W*here to begin? We are indebted to far too many people to mention.

To all those teachers and friends, pastors and leaders, authors and allies who have poured into our lives their wisdom and instruction, we thank you. And to the great company of women we are honored to call our sisters, our friends, and specifically to *all* the women who are now a part of, or who have ever been a part of Ransomed Heart; we thank you. You are *captivating*.

Thank you to our allies at Thomas Nelson. Brian, your edits and counsel have, once again, made a far better book. Mike, Jonathan, Jerry, Kyle—your vision and desire are kindling a great fire in the heart of God's people. And to our allies at Yates and Yates, samurai warriors for the Kingdom.

To those who have prayed for us through this battle. You know what it's been like.

(It feels like an Academy Awards speech, and they're now trying to get us off the stage.)

And last but not least, to the One who loves us most and best, to our amazing God, our valiant, beautiful Lord. Oh, how we adore you. This is our offering. This is our love poured out.

About the Authors

John Eldredge is the director of Ransomed Heart™ in Colorado Springs, Colorado, a fellowship devoted to helping people discover the heart of God. John is the author of numerous books, including *Epic, Waking the Dead, Wild at Heart, Walking with God, Desire,* and *Love and War* (with his wife, Stasi). John and Stasi live in Colorado; they have three sons. He loves living in the Rocky Mountains so he can pursue his other passions, including fly-fishing, mountain climbing, and exploring the waters of the West in his canoe.

Stasi Eldredge is the leader of the women's ministry of Ransomed Heart and loves the joy and freedom that comes from knowing the passionate, stunning love of Jesus Christ and lives to see others come to know him more deeply. Stasi is drawn to the beauty of the West and prefers being outside in her garden to inside tending her home. She loves her precious family, deep conversations, the wind, the woods, her dog, someone else doing the dishes, a good movie, a good cry, and "most of all, how God loves and surprises me by continuing to come for my heart in amazing and intimate ways."

To learn more about John and Stasi's ministry,
visit www.ransomedheart.com.

CAPTIVATING: HEART TO HEART SMALL GROUP VIDEO SERIES

Join Stasi Eldredge and her small group as they open their hearts, sharing with other women the deep healing and spiritual growth available by following the *Captivating* journey.

Features Include:

- ~ Five DVDs with ten 30-minute video sessions

- ~ Resource CD with a poster, bulletin inserts, invitations, encouragement cards, and facilitator's guide

CAPTIVATING: A GUIDED JOURNAL

Filled with questions and space for journaling to provoke further exploration into the image of femininity that God intended for your life.

AVAILABLE NOW
WHEREVER BOOKS ARE SOLD

FOR THE JOURNEY

DEVELOPING A CONVERSATIONAL INTIMACY WITH GOD

Developing a Conversational Intimacy with God explores why it is part of the normal Christian life to walk intimately with Christ. He longs to speak, and it is our right and privilege to hear His Voice. If you long for more in your relationship with God, you will understand "how" and "why" we are invited into the closest of fellowships with Him.

THE HOPE OF PRAYER

Things Can Be Different.

Every one of us can point to things in our lives that we'd sure like to see change. Lots of things. Relationships that need some help. Health issues. A need for guidance and direction. Financial woes . . .

The list for most of us is pretty long. And to help us bring about that change, God has given us prayer.

The Scriptures talk a lot about prayer, but we're not really sure what to do with it, or, more importantly, how to do it. At least, how to do it in a way that works. Meaning, it actually brings about change.

But that's what prayer is supposed to do! Bring about change. When Jesus teaches us to pray "Thy Kingdom come, thy will be done," he means precisely that—that our prayers somehow enable the Kingdom of God to come and his will to be done "on earth as it is in heaven."

Meaning, here, now, in our lives.

In *The Hope of Prayer* series John shares how to pray with hope and confidence—how to apply prayer to the various dilemmas of life. A live audience recording, this 8 CD set includes the question and answer period at the end of each session, as well as John fielding prayer requests and praying—providing a mini prayer clinic.

There are few thoughts as hopeful as the thought that things can be different. And so the disciples said, "Teach us to pray." We hope through this series you will find answers to many of the questions you have longed to ask.

THE UTTER RELIEF OF HOLINESS

"Long before he laid down earth's foundations, God had us in mind, had settled on us as the focus of his love, to be made whole and holy by his love." (Ephesians 1: 3–4, *The Message*)

Whole and holy. Have we ever put those two words together before? We've thought of wholeness as something for which we hope . . . that remains elusive. And as for holiness, doesn't the word sound sort of heavy and disciplined and hard?

It's not.

When we discover what the salvation of Jesus Christ means for our own restoration, we'll find that holiness is an expression of the healing of our humanity. What a relief it would be to be set free from all that plagues us: the inner struggle with anger or contempt, the struggle with habitual sins.

We can! We can be set free . . . through the healing work of Christ in our lives.

In this four-part CD series, John Eldredge explores the beauty of the genuine goodness available to us in Jesus Christ and guides us through the process whereby God makes us whole and holy by his love.

You will be relieved. Utterly.

Only Available at RansomedHeart.com!

Other Books from John Eldredge

Epic. In this retelling of the gospel in four acts, John Eldredge presents God not only as the author of life, but also as the actor in a story where the "plot" reaches the depths of our souls. Now you, too, can discover your role in the drama. This book shows how our hearts long for great drama and why the gospel is truly epic.

Waking the Dead. In *Waking the Dead,* John Eldredge shows how God restores your heart, your true humanity, and sets you free. There are four streams, Eldredge says, through which you can discover the abundant life: Walking with God, Receiving His Intimate Counsel, Deep Restoration, and Spiritual Warfare. And once the "eyes of your heart" are opened, you will embrace three eternal truths: things are not what they seem, this is a world at war, and you have a crucial role to play. A battle is raging. And it is a battle for your heart.

A Guidebook to Waking the Dead: Embracing the Life God Has for You. In a style similar to *Desire Journal and Guidebook,* Eldredge and Craig McConnell lead you on your personal journey toward a restored heart, true humanity, and ultimate freedom.

Wild at Heart. Every man was once a boy. And every little boy has dreams, big dreams. But what happens to those dreams when they grow up? In *Wild at Heart,* John Eldredge invites men to recover their masculine heart, defined in the image of a passionate God. And he invites women to discover the secret of a man's soul and to delight in the strength and wildness men were created to offer.

Wild at Heart Field Manual. Abandoning the format of workbooks-as-you-know-them, the *Wild at Heart Field Manual* will take you on a journey where you will receive permission to be what God designed you to be—dangerous, passionate, alive, and free. Filled with questions, exercises, personal stories from readers, and journal space to record your "field notes," this book will lead you on a journey to discover the masculine heart that God gave you.

Pg 49
70
76
87
114
116
117
131
134 *
135
147 *